GETTING OUT OF A CONTRACT

TO OUR WIVES AND CHILDREN

GETTING OUT OF A CONTRACT
A PRACTICAL GUIDE FOR BUSINESS

❖

Adam Rose, David Leibowitz
and Adrian Magnus

Gower

Published by
Gower Publishing Limited
Gower House
Croft Road
Aldershot
Hampshire GU11 3HR
England

Gower Publishing Company
131 Main Street
Burlington
VT 05401–5600 USA

A. Rose, D. Leibowitz and A. Magnus have asserted their right under the Copyright, Designs and Patents Act 1988 to be identified as the authors of this work.

E-mail and website addresses are correct at time of printing.

British Library Cataloguing-in-Publication Data
Rose, Adam
Getting Out of a Contract: A Practical Guide for Business
1. Discharge of contracts—England.   2. Discharge of contracts—Wales.
I. Title.   II. Leibowitz, David.   III. Magnus, Adrian.
346.4'2'022'024338

ISBN 0-566-08161-X

US Library of Congress Cataloging-in-Publication Data
Rose, Adam, 1966–
Getting Out of a Contract: A Practical Guide for Business / Adam Rose, David Leibowitz and Adrian Magnus
p.   cm.   Include index.
1. Breach of contrct—Great Britain—Popular works.   2. Business law—Great Britain.
1. Leibowitz, David, 1960–.   II. Magnus, Adrian, 1963–.   III. Title.
KD1600.Z9.R67 2001
346.4102'2–dc21
00–063639

Typeset in Garamond Light and Avant Garde Book by Acorn Bookwork, Salisbury, Wiltshire, and printed in Great Britain by TJ International Ltd, Padstow, Cornwall.

CONTENTS

PREFACE

This book has been written by three practising solicitors, each chapter written by one of us, resulting in a different style, a different approach and a different emphasis from chapter to chapter.

Some aspects of this book are, by their very nature, prone to a more traditional exposition than others and Chapter 5, in particular, dealing with the recently much changed rules surrounding competition law (or, as the Americans have it, anti-trust), has had to be less chatty than other chapters. But overall, 'chatty' has been very much our guiding aim, which we hope we have achieved.

Our aim has not been to produce a textbook for the law student, but a book for those with an interest, in a commercial setting, of how the law might help – or, indeed, hinder – them. We have tried to make the book as accessible as possible, consistent with dealing with complex legal issues. Contract law, which is very much the cornerstone of commercial law, is not an easy subject. It is generally taught to law undergraduates in their first year of study and is an essential requirement of the training required by both the solicitors' and barristers' sides of the legal profession. Commercial lawyers continue to be fascinated by its details and its difficulties throughout their careers. Contract law has also shown itself to be remarkably resilient to the onward march of the new economy; the general approach of the courts has been to recognize that however a contract comes into being, traditional contract law still provides good answers. To that end, although this book is grounded in a traditional context, its principles will (generally) apply to the on-line world of e-commerce, m-commerce and whatever comes out after that.

We have, where appropriate, used case references in the traditional legal format – the reader who is not used to such legal form might simply note the year of the case (which will generally be clear from the reference, sometimes in traditional brackets, and sometimes in square brackets – the distinction does not matter here) and not bother with the rest of the reference; the lawyer might want to follow up the reference. In any event, we have kept to using only one or two references for a case, and not used the four or five references for the same judgement that sometimes can appear. As we have tried to say, if the reader is a lawyer needing detailed case references, or someone looking for an academic text, we will only disappoint. We have, where necessary, or appropriate, used legal terms, but our hope is that they will be clearly understood, either from the context in which they are used, or because we explain them when we use them. Our general approach has been to recognize that the law is sometimes surrounded by mystery that should not be there, and so to avoid, where we can, falling into the trap of excluding the non-lawyer from what is really going on.

The genesis of this book was a series of talks given by the authors to our clients, under the general heading of 'how to get out of a contract'. An article followed, which was picked up by our publishers, and this book is an expansion of that.

We have, at various times, worried that others in our profession would be worried that anarchic lawyers were on the loose, threatening their livelihoods, but also encouraging contractual mayhem; after all, getting clients into contracts is surely what lawyers should be doing. We hope that we are not encouraging a free-for-all between contracting parties, but instead simply adding to the available stock of business books. And if a party wants to get out of a contract, we hope to be of some help.

As is usual with any book dealing with the law, we should address one fact head on: this book is not a substitute for taking specific legal advice, which the reader should always seek before deciding upon a particular course of action, or inaction. Instead, this book has been written with a view to helping businesspeople understand a bit more about the processes lawyers are going through when we are asked, 'how do I get out of a contract?'; if that understanding helps business people better address how they are to act, and the context, from a legal perspective, of where they stand and what rights (or obligations) they might have, then our job in relation to this book will have been done.

We would like to thank our wives, Nicola, Gillian and Sharon, our children, Ben, Joseph, Samantha, Jonathan, Naomi, Rachel and Gideon, our secretaries, Barbara, Julie, Jenny, Janet, our trainee solicitors who, at varying times in the writing of this book, have shared our rooms and our frustrations with the time it takes to write something, which, at the outset, seemed so simple. Most of all for all her patience shown to us, well beyond the call of duty, we owe a great thank you to Jo Burges of our publishers, Gower. Without Jo's regular, yet always polite, chasing messages, our clients, who seemed to have plotted to make time unavailable to us throughout the period of writing this book, would have won.

Finally, we have tried to state the law as we understand it at 20 May 2000. The authors are all qualified as English solicitors, which means that our competence is the law of England and Wales. Scottish and Northern Irish laws are different in many ways from English law, and this book is limited to the laws of England and Wales accordingly. Any errors are entirely ours, and any readers who believe that they have uncovered an error in this text are very much welcome to write to us, care of the publishers.

Adam Rose
David Leibowitz
Adrian Magnus

1

HOW TO GET OUT OF A CONTRACT

Lawyers are frequently asked to advise on variations of these two questions:

1   Can you help me to negotiate my way into a contract?
2   Can you help me get out of a contract that I am currently in?

The second type of question is posed just as frequently (if not more frequently) than the first. This book will, first, help you to identify whether you are in fact in a contract. We will look at some key relevant terms and laws that might help you to get out of a contract and will conclude with a review of some of the consequences of walking away from your contract should you elect to do so.

In order to help illustrate the legal issues addressed in the book, we will from time to time return to, and work through, two scenarios which are described in this chapter. We have not, simply for the sake of it, used these examples to illustrate every point we make in this book, but we do return to them regularly. We believe that they do, in large part, sum up our clients' collective experiences, although neither case is meant to reflect any actual experiences of any of our clients, nor is any name used in either case intended to be a reference to any real person or business. The first scenario concerns a supermarket that has contracted to buy baking equipment that it no longer needs or wants. The second scenario concerns a garage that has contracted to maintain a fleet of cars over a period of time. The contract is proving to be unprofitable and the garage now wishes to exit the contract early.

THE BAKERY SCENARIO

Supplier Limited (which, for the sake of brevity, we will refer to as 'Supplier') is a supplier of catering equipment. Typical clients include hospitals, schools, restaurants, staff canteens and similar types of places. For this type of client, Supplier is able to provide the full range of catering equipment required, ranging from walk-in freezers down to pots and pans.

Phil is the Managing Director of Supplier. After working for many years in the catering industry, he set up Supplier with the help of a modest bank loan ten years ago. He now has a staff of 25 and a turnover of £6m each year.

Phil has a number of contacts at National Health Service Trusts in his local area. In recent years, Supplier has supplied catering equipment to most of the hospitals, clinics and nursing homes in the local area. Supplier does not manufacture any of the equipment that it sells. Supplies are purchased directly from manufacturers and sold on by Supplier to its customers.

Phil pays his sales staff a basic salary plus commission on sales. The staff are, therefore, encouraged to seek out new business opportunities for Supplier. Over the years, Phil has come to the view that to get the best out of his sales staff, it is important to let them have a relatively free rein.

Jim is a fairly new member of the sales staff. He has only been with the company for 18 months. Jim plays football for a local Sunday league team. Over a beer after one particular match, Jim was introduced to Bill. It was a timely meeting and they found that they had a common business interest. Bill is Facilities Manager for a small supermarket chain ('Supermarket') with five local branches.

During discussions, it emerged that Supermarket is looking to start up its own on-site bakery. Currently, Supermarket buys in all bread and cakes. However, the quality is variable. Much of the produce is not as fresh as it could be and the price is too high.

Supermarket is considering a change in strategy. The purchase of sliced bread and packaged cakes will continue. However, in each of its five local stores, Supermarket wants to have the facility to be able to bake a variety of fresh bread and cakes. Hopefully, this will help to keep Supermarket's customers in the store rather than losing this business to the local bakeries. Jim has some limited knowledge about ovens for industrial use generally, although he has not previously been involved in either the purchase or sale of an oven to be used exclusively for baking purposes. Nevertheless, Jim had managed to impress Bill with some technical jargon and industry knowledge about industrial ovens generally. They agreed to keep in touch.

Jim was excited about the prospect of this potential new source of business. Supplier had never before made any sales to supermarkets. When Jim reported the lead to Phil he was delighted and directed Jim to follow it up.

Supplier purchases ovens from most of the large oven manufacturers, but has a particularly close working relationship with Manufacturer Limited ('Manufacturer'). Over the years, Supplier has found Manufacturer to be a reliable manufacturer, with competitively priced products. Because of the quantity of business that Supplier places with Manufacturer, Supplier has in the past been able to negotiate favourable discount arrangements with Manufacturer.

Jim contacted Gordon who is his opposite number at Manufacturer. At this stage, the discussions were in fairly general terms. Jim explained that he was looking to buy some baking ovens for sale to a supermarket client. Jim needed to get some idea of the type of oven that would be suitable for super-market use and the approximate cost.

Gordon reported to Jim that Manufacturer was currently in the process of developing a product ('Oven 2000') which he thought might be ideal for supermarket use. Gordon explained that the key features of the 'Oven 2000' were:

1   40 shelves (known as 'grids')
2   Wheel-in trolleys
3   Over 50 pre-set programmes
4   An easy to use and quick cleaning programme to prevent scaling
5   Sophisticated humidity controller to provide dry heat/steam/combi-nation (as required) – with ability to monitor the inherent moisture content of the food
6   Works off three-phase electricity supply or natural gas
7   Approximate cost £25 000.

The 'Oven 2000' was not yet on the market. It was currently undergoing some final testing. However, to try and place some advanced sales, Manufacturer had already produced a sales brochure about the product. Gordon gave a copy to Jim.

Jim had now identified the type of oven which he thought was probably ideally suited to the needs of a small supermarket chain. He arranged a meeting with Bill. Bill explained that matters had moved on since their last discussions. Supermarket was undergoing a re-branding procedure to coincide with the busy Christmas period. Supermarket had already launched a sizeable advertising campaign to bring the re-branding to the attention of the public. Bill explained that just within the last week a decision had been made by the Board to feature fresh bakery products in the campaign. The adver-tising agency retained by Supermarket had already been instructed to make revisions to their campaign to feature the new fresh bakery produce.

To coincide with the strategy, Bill explained that Supermarket needed baking equipment in each of its five local stores to be up and running within four weeks (that is, by 10 December). There was now limited time available to do much shopping around. Bill was pleased to learn that Jim had identified an oven that was likely to be suitable for Supermarket's needs.

In the days that followed, there were a number of discussions concerning purchase of the ovens. Gordon and Jim spoke about the terms of the proposed sale of ovens from Manufacturer to Supplier. Gordon had no direct contact with Supermarket. Jim and Bill spoke about the terms of the sale from Supplier to Supermarket.

The key features of the deal were:

1   Manufacturer would sell five 'Oven 2000' ovens to Supplier for £20 000 each, less a 10 per cent discount (total of £90 000).
2   Down payment of £50 000 by Supplier to Manufacturer on placing order. Balance to be invoiced by Manufacturer to Supplier on delivery.
3   Manufacturer to deliver directly to each of the five supermarkets.
4   Installation would be undertaken by Supermarket locally.
5   Supplier contracted to sell five 'Oven 2000' ovens to Supermarket at £25 000 each.
6   Supplier to invoice Supermarket £125 000 on delivery.
7   Key personnel at both Supplier and Manufacturer knew that Supermarket needed the ovens in place and up and running by 10 December.

The paperwork in respect of the deal was minimal. Supplier issued a purchase order to Manufacturer with its terms and conditions of purchase on the reverse side. On receipt of the purchase order, Manufacturer issued an invoice to Supplier for £90 000. The invoice read '£50 000 down payment received – balance due on delivery of ovens'. The reverse side of the invoice set out the terms and conditions of sale of Manufacturer.

Supermarket sent a purchase order to Supplier. The order read, 'For supply of 5 "Oven 2000" @ £25 000 each to be invoiced on delivery. Delivery required by 10 December'. The reverse side of the purchase order set out Supermarket's terms and conditions of purchase.

On delivery of ovens no. 4 and 5, Supplier submitted an invoice in respect of all five ovens to Supermarket for £125 000. The invoice carried Supplier's standard terms and conditions of sale on the reverse side.

Manufacturer knew that the delivery dates were likely to be tight. The prototype of 'Oven 2000' was still undergoing the final stages of testing when the order was placed. The factory workers at Manufacturer's premises were required to put in a significant amount of overtime in order to complete the order.

The run-up to the Christmas period proved to be highly problematic for all three parties. Manufacturer was working to full capacity on production of the five ovens. Each of the ovens was delivered to the local supermarket branch when it came off the production line.

The first two ovens were delivered prior to 10 December. However, from the moment of installation, there were problems with both ovens. Both were functional in the sense that edible bread and cakes could be baked using the ovens. However, Supermarket was experiencing two practical problems. First, rough and ready manual settings had to be used because the automatic programmes were proving to be unreliable. Second, one of the ovens was scaling up and was proving difficult and time-consuming to clean.

Supermarket made direct contact with Manufacturer in an effort to get the problems resolved and to try to speed up production of the other three ovens.

Supermarket considered that it had no alternative but to continue to bake with the two ovens that had been supplied although the produce was far from the quality expected and the cleaning time between baking sessions was excessive. Oven no. 3 was in working order and was delivered on 10 December.

Ovens no. 4 and 5 were available for delivery on 20 December and were delivered to site. However, there was simply no time to get those bakeries up and running before the New Year period. Staff and management were simply too busy.

In the first week of January, Supermarket management re-grouped to review business over the Christmas period and trading generally. One of the items for consideration was to review how the bakeries had performed. The Regional Director reported that there had been quite serious teething problems with the 'Oven 2000' product and that late delivery of ovens 4 and 5 had resulted in two local branches being unable to fulfil promises to customers to provide local bakery produce on site. However, most of the discussions centred upon a review of the in-house bakery strategy generally rather than the more specific problem with the ovens. The evidence suggested that contrary to their initial research, the local Supermarket branches would be unable to compete with the long-established local bakeries. A Board decision was taken to scrap the in-house bakery project.

Bill received a memorandum from the Board with instructions to require the Supplier/Manufacturer to take back all five ovens. The ovens were no longer required. The Supermarket had paid nothing for the ovens as yet and intended to pay nothing for them. Supplier had agreed to invoice Supermarket only after delivery of the ovens. Jim had not been able to negotiate any advanced payment from Supermarket at the time the contract was made. Supermarket was an important new client. Supermarket dictated the terms and would not agree to be invoiced until delivery. Although all ovens have now been delivered, Supplier has not yet received any payment from Supermarket. Bill has made it clear to Jim that Supermarket does not intend to make any payment whatsoever.

Jim consults Phil. Phil is furious that Supplier now finds itself in such an exposed position. He takes control of the position himself and sends a firm letter to Supermarket threatening legal action if £125 000 is not paid within

14 days. The letter states that Supermarket contracted to buy five ovens from Supplier at an agreed price. The ovens have been delivered but no payment has been made.

Bill's instructions from Head Office are clear. There is no further need for the ovens. They should be collected by the Supplier/Manufacturer and under no circumstances is any payment to be made to the Supplier/Manufacturer.

Bill needs legal advice to find out where Supermarket stands in relation to the demand for payment. He knows that Supermarket has contracted to buy five ovens that it no longer needs or wants.

Phil also needs legal advice. He wants to avoid falling out with Supermarket, but Supplier is coming under pressure from Manufacturer to pay the £40 000 balance of the purchase price that fell due upon delivery. Supplier, remember, is already £50 000 out of pocket having paid a deposit to Manufacturer when it ordered the ovens.

THE GARAGE SCENARIO

George owns and manages a medium-sized garage near the town centre called 'Rapid Repairs'. The garage has a good selection of new and nearly new Vauxhalls and Fords for sale. It also carries out MOT tests, repairs and services, mainly on Vauxhalls and Fords.

A car rental business called 'Rent a Car Limited' has recently opened in the town. Max is the proprietor. George has been trying to persuade Max to buy some of his cars.

George has a good selection of cars and they are competitively priced. Max tells George that he is not looking to add any more cars to his fleet just yet. However, as and when he does, he hopes to be able to place some orders with George.

Max does, however, need to get his cars serviced and valeted on a regular basis and, of course, from time to time, mechanical and/or bodywork repairs are required to be carried out.

Preferably, Max wants to work with one garage only. He is looking to place a block maintenance contract with one garage in return for a fixed annual maintenance fee. If terms can be agreed, Max would like to place the business with George.

George knows that it is important that he strikes a sensible deal with Max if he can. There are a number of garages in town and if George does not do a deal, another garage will step in. However, George needs to ensure that if he is going to offer to Max a range of services for a fixed fee, the fee has to be pitched at the right level to ensure that it is economical for his garage to carry out the work.

George knows that Max currently has a fleet of 50 hire cars. They are all either Vauxhalls or Fords. Max wants each car comprehensively serviced once a year and valeted each time a car is returned. Max also wants the cars repaired as and when required.

The frequency and cost of repairs is difficult for George to predict but George is prepared for his garage to do these repairs as part of the package.

Max is prepared to spend an annual budget of £20 000 on garage costs. Max is looking for Rent a Car to enter into a contract with Rapid Repairs guaranteeing to the garage a regular income of £20 000 per annum for each of the five years. If all goes well, after the first year, Max hopes that his business will expand and expects to buy cars for his new fleet from George.

George is particularly attracted by the prospect of a regular income stream which should help his cash flow. He is hopeful that if Rapid Repairs perform well, it could be the start of a profitable long-term relationship with Rent a Car.

Max and George shake hands on a deal over lunch and Max writes to confirm the terms the following day. His letter reads as follows:

Rapid Repairs Limited
31 High Street
Tadworth

Dear George
Rent a Car Limited
I am writing to confirm terms agreed between Rent a Car Limited and Rapid Repairs Limited at our meeting yesterday. The terms are as follows:

1   This agreement commences today.
2   It will continue for five years after which either of us can end it on 90 days' notice.
3   Rapid Repairs will service and valet all hire cars belonging to Rent a Car on request.
4   Cars to be returned serviced and/or valeted within one working day of delivery.
5   Repairs to cars to be undertaken by Rapid Repairs as and when requested. Return of car upon repair to be agreed on a case by case basis.
6   Rent a Car will pay to Rapid Repairs £20 000 each year on a quarterly basis (that is, a quarter of the charge on first day of March, June, September and December) for each year of this contract.
7   Spare parts to be invoiced by Rapid Repairs to Rent a Car at cost.

Please confirm that these terms are agreed by sending a signed copy of this letter back to me.
Yours sincerely

Max

Although the terms fell in line with the key factors that George and Max discussed over lunch, George never did countersign the letter. In fact, he never even answered the letter. Nevertheless, in the month that followed, Rent a Car did indeed begin to send its cars round to Rapid Repairs. Quarterly payments were made but much to George's aggravation every payment was always at least six weeks late.

Towards the end of the first year George was becoming a little concerned about the arrangement with Max. Despite the various assurances that had been given, Max had not in fact bought any cars at all from George. However, the size of the fleet was growing. Max had been buying cars from one of George's rivals. As the size of the fleet grew the demands upon Rapid Repairs grew and the profitability of the contract decreased.

George was turning away a good deal of business that was potentially more lucrative than the Rent a Car deal because of his commitments on the Rent a Car contract.

However, matters came to a head 18 months into the contract. George read in his local paper that Rent a Car had taken over the business of the only other rental company in town. Overnight, the Rent a Car fleet had doubled.

George rang Max the following day to congratulate him on the deal and to discuss the new arrangements that George expected that he and Max would now have to negotiate. As the size of the fleet had now doubled overnight, George was looking for the annual maintenance fee to be significantly increased. In addition to the increase in the size of the fleet, a large number of the new cars were German and Japanese. Although George's staff would be able to service and repair these cars, his staff were less familiar with these cars than the Vauxhalls and Fords upon which they worked every day.

Max told George not to worry. The acquisition was good news for Rapid Repairs he said. He hoped that the growth of Rent a Car would help Rapid Repairs to grow.

However Max stated quite plainly that for the duration of the remainder of the contract (approximately three and a half years) there would be no increase to the annual maintenance fee. He accepted that the workload on Rapid Repairs would double now that the fleet had doubled in size but Max said that the initial maintenance fee was never linked to the size of the fleet. George considers that Max has been unscrupulous. George was struggling to perform the Rent a Car contract at a profitable level even prior to the takeover. After the takeover, George knows that the contract is bound to be loss-making.

George has decided that he no longer trusts Max. He can see no business future in the relationship and having failed to re-negotiate terms, he wants to terminate the arrangement.

2

IS THERE A CONTRACT?

BACKGROUND

From Chapter 3 onwards we will be looking at the different weapons you might be able to use to get out of an agreement. In this chapter we address the fundamental question of whether there is a contract at all; for if there is no contract, you do not need this book. The remaining chapters of this book work on the assumption that there is, indeed, a contract in place, but the very first issue for a lawyer to determine is whether that assumption can be made. The aim of this chapter is not to turn every reader into a contracts lawyer, but to help explain what a contract is (from a legal point of view), and so help set the stage for the remainder of this book.

If there is no contract at all, then unless some other branch of law requires one to do, or not do, something – in varying degrees of seriousness, you must not kill or steal, or jump red lights, or tell tales, or wipe your nose on your sleeve – the absence of a contract means that some other person cannot force you to do, or not do, that thing.

WHAT IS A CONTRACT?

One of the leading academic books on the law of contract defines a contract as 'an agreement giving rise to obligations which are enforced or recognised by law'.[1] All very well, but faced with the question 'do I have to pay for that?' or 'do I have to do this?', this book is not intended to address the academic arguments surrounding philosophical questions of what is a contract. Readers wishing to read the academic texts should consider any of the books mentioned in the Bibliography.

Instead, this book will work from the premise that if the thing meets the requirements of a contract, then that is a contract (or, as they say, 'if it waddles like a duck, quacks like a duck, and looks like a duck … it's a duck!'). Put simply, once the reader has reached the end of this chapter, its authors' hope is that the answer to whether or not there is a contract will be clearer. If that does not sound very ambitious, remember that undergraduate law students often spend a whole year on basic contract law, and as long again on various sub-sets of the species. Contract law is one of the fundamental cornerstones of modern life – society, as we know it, would be different (and some might say simpler and more pleasant) if, instead of contract law, we were simply honourable people, who relied on our moral standing, shame and goodwill to get things done, from buying our milk and bread for breakfast, and our transport to work and everything we do there. But, as even a rudimentary bartering system relies on contract law to regulate things, contract law has evolved into a highly complex regime of interweaving rules. We hope to have highlighted the main issues here, and to have provided some signposts and other markings along the way.

All contracts have certain essential features: an offer and an acceptance (and these two features are sometimes reduced to the single essential requirement of an 'agreement' – for an agreement is precisely that: an offer which is accepted); consideration (which is a legally technical term, explained later in this chapter); and an intention to create legal relations. All these essential features have to be present or else there is no contract – an intention to create legal relations is not a contract if no agreement is present (if we intend to have a contract, but fail to agree any terms, it is no surprise that there is no contract); and an agreement with no intention to create legal relations is no contract either (so, if we agree to meet at the pub, only in quite exceptional circumstances – such as, you, the pub landlord have employed me to do bar work – will there be any doubt that there is no contract).

The traditional view is that because the absence of any of the essential features means that there is no contract, each of the essential features is of equal importance. In this chapter, we will start by looking at intention to create legal relations, then look at offer and acceptance, and end with consideration.

INTENTION TO CREATE LEGAL RELATIONS

If the parties sign an express contract, it can generally be taken that they have intended to enter into a contract. Obviously, not all contracts are so clear-cut (as, for example, taken in isolation, might be said of the letter from Max to George), and as one of the purposes of this chapter is to help identify ways of not being caught in a contract, we will be concentrating on the less clear-cut situations that frequently arise. So, when Max wrote to George after their lunch, asking George to send a signed copy of his letter back to Max, as confirmation that the terms as set out in the letter were agreed, a clear contractual intention was being laid out for all to see. The courts have made clear that if one side argues that it had not intended to enter into a legally binding contract, the courts should remember that 'contracts are not lightly to be implied'. In other words, the party wanting to enforce its contractual rights will have to prove that there is a contract. How?

A leading nineteenth-century case makes clear that the courts normally apply an objective test – that is, does it appear to the reasonable person that there was an intention to create legal relations? The reason for the test is clearly that, if Supermarket relied on the objective appearance of Supplier having an intention to create legal relations, then Supplier has to comply with the contract terms even if (unknown to Supermarket), Supplier (so as to speak) had his fingers crossed at the time! This book is not meant as an anarchist's charter, nor as a Marxist's analysis of the role of contract law in the ways of a capitalist economy – but, to be quite clear, unless certain rules of the game were set down, capitalism would have struggled! In other words, the courts have, over time, developed various devices to help build confidence in the system we now know as contract law, and perhaps the most famous device of all is that of the 'reasonable person' (or, in older times, the 'reasonable man'). That person, whom readers might also know as 'the man on the Clapham omnibus', acts as the hidden umpire, called in to help decide whether, on balance and objectively, a legal construction can, or cannot, be made out. If, throughout this book, the reader stops to ask him or herself whether the conclusion we (and the courts) are reaching seems right or wrong, please consider what the man on that bus might be thinking – his answer, in light of the explanations we attempt to give here, should match what the reader (on reflection) would expect.

There are a number of legal devices that are used to make clear that, at any given stage before a contract is made, there is no intention (at that stage) to make a legally binding deal. The most well-known such device is the 'subject to contract' marking of any document that could be a contract. Anyone who has ever bought or sold a house or flat will have seen that phrase used on every document (letters, draft contracts, preliminary enquiries and replies to preliminary enquiries) until exchange. Other devices include making clear on the document that it is 'not intended to be legally binding' (in which case, one might note, why agree its terms at all?) Or that it is 'only an expression of intention and not a legal agreement'. Documents headed as 'memorandum of understanding', 'heads of agreement' or similar such things might, or might not, be legally binding – it all depends on whether, objectively tested, there was an intention to create legal relations (and the other key requirements, of offer, acceptance and consideration, are met). These issues and devices are all dealt with in more detail in Chapter 9.

The type of situation that sometimes leads to the most acrimonious of disputes involves agreements between family members – parents can make legally binding contracts with their children (as long as the child is 18 or older, or if younger, depending on the circumstances: so, a 5-year-old can contract to buy a lollipop, and a 10-year-old can buy a bus ticket; but a 7-year-old cannot buy land).

The bottom line is that the presence, or absence, of an intention to create contractual relations is a question to be decided objectively, and the factual circumstances surrounding that will determine whether it was (objectively) right that one party understood the other to intend to enter into legal relations.

OFFER

An offer is usually presented as the starting point of any contract. It is, as any plain English reading of the word would anticipate, a statement of what one party is willing to do, or pay or promise, in exchange for some act, payment, or promise of the person (or class of people – such as bidders in an auction) to whom the statement is made.

An offer has a clear legal status – it is something which is designed to be capable of acceptance, without ambiguity, discussion or counter-proposal, by the other person. It is more than a preliminary part of the pre-contract skirmishes between people thinking about contracting. Those skirmishes usually involve one party asking if the other might be willing to pay a price, say, for a house (the enquiry being made by way of estate agents' particulars), and the other proposing a suggested price at which he would buy. That reply, assuming it is worded along the lines of 'subject to my survey and us agreeing the legal terms', is an offer (albeit, conditional, in the example just given, of satisfactory survey and legal terms being settled). In the case of the house purchase, the seller makes what lawyers call an 'invitation to treat' – she invites interested third parties to make an offer to her, which she may accept or reject. The prospective buyer, invited by the estate agent to see the house, makes an offer. The usual ritual then sees the seller making a counter-offer; that is, the buyer's offered price is too low, and the seller reduces the original asking price by way of a counter-offer of a price higher than that offered by the buyer. At the other extreme, no one (although we all probably know the exception to this rule) tries to negotiate on the price of their morning newspaper. The fact that some statement includes the word 'offer' proves nothing: there are two standard situations in which the non-lawyer could anticipate that an offer is being made by the seller, whereas on close inspection, and in light of the discussion just presented, that turns out not to be the case.

The first situation is in an auction. The seller is offering to sell his painting to the highest bidder. In fact, in law, the seller is inviting bids, and it is the bidder who makes the offer, which the auctioneer accepts on behalf of the seller by banging his hammer.

The second situation is that of the display of products in a shop window. They might even proclaim 'special offer'. The display does not constitute an offer, but is an invitation to a buyer to make an offer to the shopkeeper to buy those products at that price. Where goods are displayed on a self-service display, again, the shopkeeper is inviting offers to buy his goods, and the shopper makes the offer (in the legal sense) when he allows them to be scanned at the checkout desk.

One other area worth mentioning is this: we often read of a company making an 'offer' of its shares to the public. In fact, the company is not (in law) doing any such thing: it is simply inviting the public to make offers for the shares.

One old case that every lawyer learns early on in any course on contract law is that of *Carlill* v. *Carbolic Smoke Ball Company*.[2] There, an advert for the smoke ball company's product (a carbolic smoke ball – few lawyers have sought to ask what that was!) promised to pay £100 (this, in the 1890s) to any user of the smoke ball who caught the flu. The court held that that advertisement was an offer (made all the more so as the advertisers promised to have deposited £1000 in the bank, so 'showing our sincerity'). The statement had been made, the court decided, with the clear intention to be bound by its promise. So, offers from newspapers for information leading to the conviction of a killer, or from the owner of a cat for its return, are all enforceable in law as contracts, accepted by the informant or cat returner.

However, a general advert – offering goods for sale – is not an offer, nor is a menu pushed through your door from your local takeaway. Other laws (such as trade descriptions laws enforced through local authorities) might impact on those things.

The problem, fascinating though it might be, is that the distinction between an offer and an invitation to treat is determined in every case on the basis of the intention of the party making the offer (or invitation to treat). When Manufacturer gave Supplier a sales brochure in respect of brand new 'Oven 2000s', that brochure does not amount in law to being an offer to sell 'Oven 2000s', but is simply background promotional material, inviting Supplier to offer to buy – even though both parties knew that they wanted to sell (or buy) those very ovens.

Offers can be made orally, in writing, or by conduct – although it will be rare that conduct alone would be enough to convince the other party that an offer was being made, let alone a judge. Obviously, if I am talking to you, there is little room to argue over questions such as where and when was the offer by me made to you. There might be grounds for disputing whether what I said amounted to an offer (in law) or not, but we have seen that, essentially, that is an objective issue for the court to determine in light of all the evidence given to the judge. But where we are not in the same room, talking to each other, we are most likely (and traditionally, only) to be corresponding with each other. The vagaries of the postal services have helped the law's development significantly in the areas of 'offer', and, as we shall see, 'acceptance'.

Offers which are posted are made, according to the (rather old) cases, where they are posted. And offers are made when they should have been received by the person to whom they are addressed. In the age of e-mail, it is generally accepted that the postal rules apply: in other words, the offer is made where I e-mail the offer from, and the offer is made when you should receive it (that is, pretty much instantaneously).

Offers can be withdrawn, or can lapse, and the general rule is that they may be withdrawn at any time before they are accepted by the other party. In fact, the withdrawal must have been received by the other party before the offer was accepted – so, in one case, an offer, which was posted on 1 October in Cardiff and reached New York on 11 October, where it was accepted at once, had been withdrawn by a further letter posted on 8 October, but the withdrawal was not received until some time after the acceptance. In that case, although the person making the offer had clearly no intention to create legal regulations by the time the acceptance was made, the offer had not been successfully withdrawn, and the court found that a contract had been made.

ACCEPTANCE

The 'acceptance' is the flip side of the offer. Unless and until there is an acceptance, the offer (unless expressed to be non-retractable) may be withdrawn, and there is no contract. The test that a court would apply to a statement to decide if it amounted to an acceptance is essentially the same test that it would apply to decide if something amounted to an offer: the objective intention to be bound by the statement is key.

Acknowledging safe receipt of an offer is not an acceptance, nor even is saying 'I accept your offer' if, on any reasonable interpretation, the offer was to do one of two things – such as (to make up an example) build a house for £100 000 or buy a racehorse for that sum – what offer would I be accepting?

Difficulties will most likely arise in those situations in which the parties have engaged in negotiations – a number of statements will have been made, some amounting to offers (or counter-offers), but some simply seeking clarifications, or making demands for better offers. It can often then happen that while one party is pleased commercially with the deal it strikes, the other seeks to argue that there is no contract at all. The court is called in to resolve the dispute, and will look at all the correspondence and notes of meetings – the judge is likely to find that a contract was made if, looked at objectively, an agreement had been reached. That will be particularly the case where one party has already performed its side of the deal.

Offers (which, we have seen, can be made by word of mouth, in written form, or, less usually, by conduct) can be accepted in those ways too. Indeed, acceptance by conduct is quite common – I order something from you, say bulbs and seeds for my garden from your catalogue, which you accept by posting them to me. Supermarket sent its purchase order to Manufacturer, requiring the five ovens by 10 December. Manufacturer delivered three on time, without ever having formally accepted the offer to buy as set out in the purchase order – objectively, there could be little doubt that the offer was accepted, and it was accepted by Manufacturer's conduct, rather than in any more formal way. It would make no sense, commercially, for you to write to me accepting my offer, or even to telephone me; sending me the seeds and bulbs is what I expect. Conversely, if I invite you to send me some goods on a sale or return basis, your sending them to me amounts to an offer, and my sale of them (and, probably, any other act which is inconsistent with your continued ownership of them – such as stamping my name on the inside cover, or lending them to my friend) amounts to an acceptance of your offer.

In any case, my conduct in relation to the goods, or yours in relation to the seeds and bulbs, only counts as acceptance if I (or you) intended it to amount to an acceptance.

In Chapter 4 we will briefly see how the law (Parliament and the courts) have striven to fill the gaps which have been caused by the parties just getting on and doing things – and that includes cases in which even the price has not been settled, but nonetheless a contract has been made.

CONSIDERATION

To be enforceable, one party's promise can only be enforced if the other provides some consideration (or value) for it. Without consideration, a promise might well carry some moral weight, and a good person might well do whatever they promised they would do, but a promise, standing alone, is not an enforceable contract. For example, if you offer to do something, which I accept and both of us intend that to be legally binding, without consideration, that promise is not enforceable under contract law.

So what is consideration? Put simply (if unhelpfully), consideration is the price that Max must pay for George's promise to carry out the work in servicing the fleet. That price can take many forms, and, obviously, money is a good form. But consideration need not be in cash; it could be a return promise to do something, or not to do something, or it could be a thing, rather than cash. In short, consideration can be anything, as long as it is something – so a 'peppercorn rent' can be just that: something as worthless as a peppercorn. There are exceptions to this rule, but for these purposes, the legal saying that 'consideration must be sufficient, but need not be adequate' (that is, it must have some legal value, but need not be of any commercial value), is probably adequate.

The exceptions include those situations where there is some undue influence or other pressure on one of the parties, with the result that the consideration accepted by that party is held by a court to be too inadequate for its promise. Courts do not often find undue influence to exist. If there has been a very bad deal struck, the courts can find there to have been an 'inconsiderable bargain', but, again, that will only apply to very few situations.

Under Acts of Parliament, contracts can be set aside in a few, limited, circumstances. These include contracts made for inadequate consideration by the maker of a promise that becomes insolvent shortly after making its deal. And extortionate credit agreements can be set aside. Consideration must relate to something yet to happen. I cannot rely on having already done something to be consideration for your new promise to do something. Say, George had, in order to impress Max, valeted Max's whole fleet with no agreement as to price, if Max then refused to pay George for this work, George would have no recourse as there was no good consideration.

Consideration must not be illegal or contrary to public policy – my promise to sell you controlled drugs will not be enforceable by you (through the courts!), whatever amount of money you propose to pay me.

There is one significant (if not quaint) exception to the key requirement of consideration: if a promise is made in a deed which is properly executed, no consideration is needed, and the promise is enforceable. There is an academic argument that a deed is not, in fact, a contract at all (as it lacks the fourth key requirement of a contract!), but in getting out of an agreement, the promisor under a deed is unlikely to care about that argument!

CERTAINTY

We have stated that to be an enforceable contract, the agreement must contain the four key requirements of offer, acceptance, consideration and intention to create legal relations, and that the absence of any of those requirements means that there is no contract.

In fact, there is one other fundamental issue, which we have been taking for granted: that there is an agreement at all. If an agreement is to be legally enforceable, its essential terms must have been agreed, or else a court cannot enforce it. That stated, where it is obvious, or there is evidence, as to what any unstated essential terms are, the courts are willing to read those unstated parts into the agreement. Courts recognize that business people are not all trained lawyers, and earn their living not from drawing up detailed contracts but by doing business – those two things, in the ideal world, will coincide, but do not always do so. Even a failure to agree the price is not necessarily going to mean that there is no contract, as (although on first stating so, it seems wrong) the price is not always an essential term – many professional services cannot be costed until after they have been performed, for example, where the basis of the charging is on a time and materials basis. Garage agreed to service all the cars in Max's fleet – George did not know how many cars there were, or would be, in the fleet, but that does not mean that there was not the necessary certainty: all the cars had to be serviced.

In addition, even if all the essential terms are covered, but are expressed so unclearly that they cannot be enforced, there is no binding contract. If the court can find a way to enforce the agreement, it will do so, however, and in one case[3] a contract in 1930 gave the buyer an option to buy a further 100 000 pieces of timber 'of fair specification' the following year. In light of the parties' previous dealings, the court was willing to decide what 'of fair specification' meant here. Finally agreements to agree are not binding. In another case[4] the House of Lords confirmed that an agreement to negotiate in good faith was not enforceable – as one Lord put it, because 'a duty to carry on negotiations in good faith is inherently repugnant. Each party is entitled to pursue his (or her) own interest … A duty to negotiate in good faith is … unworkable in practice.'

NOTES

1   Treitel, G. H. (1995), *The Law of Contract*, 10th edn, London: Sweet and Maxwell.
2   *Carlill* v. *Carbolic Smoke Ball Company* [1893] 1 QB 256.
3   *Hillas* v. *Arcos* [1932] All ER 494.
4   *Walford* v. *Miles* [1992] 2 AC 128.

3

ARE YOU A PARTY TO THE CONTRACT?

This chapter addresses a number of issues, all of which should be seen in many ways to be part of the preliminary investigations that the lawyer will go through to get to a position where the client can be advised. The chapter looks at identifying the parties, assessing if the current parties are the same as the original ones, and ends with a summary of a new law that is changing one of the fundamental foundations of English contract law.

WHO ARE YOU?

So, who are you? If that sounds like an odd question, consider the garage scenario. As we know, George owns and manages a town centre garage called 'Rapid Repairs'. Without adding any complications to the core facts, with whom has Rent a Car Limited contracted?

If Rapid Repairs is simply a trading name of George's business, the contract is with George, who, in that case, is a sole trader. If George (despite telling us that he 'owns' the garage) is in fact the main owner, but some of the business is owned by someone else, Rapid Repairs is a partnership, which can itself contract. But Rapid Repairs might be the trading name of a company, wholly owned by George (or by George and others), called Rapid Repairs Limited – in which case Rapid Repairs Limited will be the contracting party. To complicate things (as so often happens in the real world), Rapid Repairs might be the trading name of a company called something completely different (such as George Limited).

If the possibility of a person being the contracting party is first considered, let us consider the common situation of a family going to a restaurant for a meal. Let us imagine that it is George's family, and he pays for the meal for himself, his wife and children. His wife develops food poisoning. The restaurant argues that its contract is with George and not his wife. In a case decided on very similar facts to these, the judge held that, despite any legal niceties and technicalities, there was a contract between the restaurant and each diner, and so each diner could sue for breach of contract if he or she suffered food poisoning. And the corollary is that if George could not pay for the meal, the restaurant could sue each diner for the price! The difficulty with this interpretation is that while it is helpful in the case of George's wife, it remains unclear what would be the case in respect of George's children – say, aged 5 and 8 – could the restaurant sue them for the money for the meal, or are they too young to make contracts, and if they are too young to be forced to pay, are they too young to sue for their food poisoning? Unfortunately, there is no clear-cut answer, but the best view would be that a child can buy sweets, but not a car, and where things fall in between those two extremes, unless there is some legislation dealing with the issue – lottery tickets, cigarettes, tickets for X-rated films – common sense will have to step in.

How can you find out whether 'Rapid Repairs' is a limited company or not? All business letters of Rapid Repairs should state its full name and address – and if it is a limited company, its registered office and company number; if it is a partnership, a full list of partners' names should be set out, or a statement showing where that list may be inspected. But not all businesses comply with those laws. You could carry out a search at Companies House (in London, Cardiff or over the Internet), but that will not necessarily give you the answer – a company does not have to trade from its registered office, which might be the office of the company's lawyers or accountants, and does not file details of its trading premises' addresses. There is, perhaps remarkably, given the number of partnerships and other forms of business operating in the UK which are not limited companies, no central register of business names or of partnerships.

CONTRACTING WITH A COMPANY

A company, as such, cannot do anything – that is, to be less dramatic and, on reflection, obvious, it is simply a legal entity, but its every action is undertaken in its name and for its benefit or detriment, by its staff and its directors.

The law has been made significantly simpler in recent years, so that now, when contracting with a company, you are entitled to assume that the person agreeing the contract on the company's behalf has the power to agree such a contract on behalf of the company, and that the company has the power to do that which it is being contracted to do. One word of warning: it has to be reasonable for you to be able to rely on the fact that the person you are negotiating with has the power to bind the company to a contract. Let us consider some examples: the service desk receptionist at a car repair garage can bind the company to repair your car at a given time for a given price; the receptionist at a law firm cannot be expected to give you legal advice on the law firm's behalf. The multinational company's board of directors would need to approve a multibillion pound purchase; the night porter could not. But the night porter could be reasonably expected to have authority to call out the premises security company, without having to wake up a director of the company in the middle of the night for approval, even though each call-out carries a fee, payable by the company.

ASSIGNMENT

Let us suppose that we have managed to identify that the Rapid Repairs that agreed to service the cars was indeed a limited company called Rapid Repairs Limited, and its registered office was at 31 High Street, Tadworth. Let us also suppose that, in addition to the facts given in Chapter 1, George owns another company, Rapid.com Limited, which sells car accessories and warranties over the Internet, and he had agreed a few months ago with Max (or, rather, Rent a Car Limited) that he (or, rather, Rapid Repairs Limited) would transfer Rapid Repairs' business into Rapid.com.

That transfer would generally be thought of as an 'assignment', although, from a lawyer's perspective, an assignment, in fact, falls short of what we will assume the various parties intended. 'Assignment' is a term used to mean the transfer of rights under a contract – so, (generally) without needing your agreement, in the absence of a prohibition in our contract on me assigning my rights under our contract, I can assign my rights under our contract to my wife. The type of right I would most commonly assign would be a right to be paid by you, and I might sell that right to a better debt collector than me; the benefit to me being that I get some percentage of what you owe me now (from the debt collector's own pocket), and the debt collector then seeks full payment from you.

But what, we are supposing, happened with Rapid Repairs is that the whole business was being transferred into Rapid.com – to achieve that, all of Rapid Repairs Limited, Rapid.com Limited and Rent a Car Limited have to agree to the transfer, and that agreement has to have all of the requirements of a contract (see Chapter 2) if it is to work. As with any contract, there is no need for this contract (known by lawyers as a 'novation') to be in writing, or to have any particular formalities, although (as ever) getting all the terms down in writing can only help when someone wants to be able to re-create the whole story, and the people involved at the time are either no longer around, or disagree as to what happened.

In fact, a novation actually creates a new contract between (in our example) Rapid.com and Rent a Car, and the contract between Rent a Car and Rapid Repairs is discharged (see Chapter 4). So, if there was a novation, the person with whom Rent a Car has its contract is Rapid.com Limited, and it is to Rapid.com, and not George or Rapid Repairs that Rent a Car should be looking for contractual performance. But, say there had been an assignment (in other words, the transfer had merely been agreed by George's two companies), would that effectively transfer the responsibilities or obligations (and not just the rights) of Rapid Repairs to Rapid.com? Generally, the answer is no, and any assignor in those circumstances would remain liable to the other party (here, Rent a Car), for any non-performance of its (that is, Rapid Repairs') obligations, until the contract comes to its end. Lawyers say that the benefit of a contract can pass to the assignee (such as the right to be paid), but without the consent of the other party (effectively, by way of a novation), the burden cannot – because I contracted to pay you for your services, not those of someone else to whom you attempt to shunt the obligation.

One further point on the question of liability: if Rapid Repairs was, in fact, a partnership – say George and his neighbour were the two partners who owned the business – each of the partners (according to the 1890 Partnership Act which still governs this issue) is 'liable jointly with the other partners' under each contract entered into by the firm while that person is a partner, whether or not that particular partner has actual knowledge of that actual contract. A partner becomes liable for all of her firm's obligations and liabilities from the moment she becomes a partner (or is held out as a partner and acquiesces to being so held out) until such time as she (or, more commonly, the firm) notifies creditors (and the world at large) that she is no longer a partner. That does not mean that the partner ceases to be liable for debts incurred while she is a partner, only that she is not liable for new debts incurred after her retirement.

AGENTS AND PRINCIPALS

You might buy something directly from the seller, or you might buy it from the seller's agent. This section looks at that second situation, where an intermediary of some description or other is involved.

The core fact is this from a legal perspective: the agent is not actually a party to the sale contract. The agent might sign the deal, or shake hands on it, and bind her principal in some other way, but, in her role as agent, she is not a contracting party.

The classic agency example that most readers will have come across in their private lives is that of the estate agent. The estate agent is not the property's owner and seller, but acts with the owner's authority to find a buyer and negotiate various aspects of the sale. But very rarely does the estate agent have the power to sign contracts on behalf of the true owner. A travel agent, on the other hand, usually does conclude contracts for the tour operator, having marketed the holiday or other travel arrangement, negotiated a price (within certain parameters, either agreed in advance with the tour operator or within the travel agent's own commission band) and sold the package – the agent does not, in that case, formally go back to the tour operator for a formal acceptance of the holiday-planner's offer to buy the particular holiday.

We have already seen the key issue in the limited examples just given: the agent must be appointed (or, at least objectively, appear to have been appointed) by the person for whom he is acting (known as the principal), and, as with any such arrangement, the contract appointing the agent can come in all shapes and sizes, or none.

This section is not designed to be a thesis on the laws governing relations between agents and their principals, but it is important to recognize, when dealing with an agent, that, first, the agent's authority might be limited by the terms of the agent's appointment, and, second, the agent is required to act in the best interests of the principal – that is, a seller's agent is acting for the seller, and not for you, the buyer, however friendly, charming and convincing the agent seems to be! More central to this chapter is the question of relations between the principal and the buyer, which is how the situation has been contemplated in this section – but the reader should recognize that the principal might just as likely be a buyer, such as an employer who is looking for new staff and engages a recruitment agent, or a business that is looking for new premises and engages a surveyor. The principal is legally responsible for all of the acts (and omissions) of the agent – but with the limitation that that statement is only true in respect of the acts of the agent which come within the agent's authority.

Where an agent's authority is limited in some way, any acts of the agent which go beyond those limits count to bind the principal – but with a clear proviso: that is only the case where the third party (the buyer from, or seller to, the principal) has, or ought to have, notice of that limitation, although, in the general run of things, one has to recognize that if something feels wrong, it might well be wrong, and further enquiry is advisable (so if it seems unlikely that the person with whom you are dealing has the level of authority they claim to have, it can only be sensible to make some enquiries to collaborate their claim and not only rely on that person's assertion that they do, indeed, have that authority).

The general rule, then, should be clear: if you contract with someone who is another person's agent, your contract is, in fact, with that other person – whether or not you have ever met or heard of that person. There are exceptions to this general statement, that most usually encountered being where, in good faith, you contract with someone who is an agent, but who has convinced you that they are acting as a principal – which might happen where they talk of 'my car' or 'my shares' or 'my services'. In that case, the position is more complicated: if the identity of the agent is important (say, you contract for the agent's services), then you have no contract with the principal; but if the importance of the contract relates to goods, rather than the identity of the seller, then the contract will be between the principal and you.

Correctly identifying the position is, therefore, critical to determining who is a party to the particular contract.

THE CONTRACTS (RIGHTS OF THIRD PARTIES) ACT 1999

The Contracts (Rights of Third Parties) Act 1999 came into force on 11 November 1999, and significantly reforms a long-standing rule known as 'privity of contract'. Under that rule, it has long been the case that a contract cannot be enforced by a person who is not a party to the contract, even though the contract is made for that person's benefit. Although the Act came into force in November 1999, it only has an impact on contracts made after six months from that date (and contracts made during those six months which expressly state that the Act was to apply to those contracts).

There have been exceptions to the old rule. For example, as we had just seen, an assignee of the benefit of a contract (such as the right to recover a debt) can enforce the contract against the other party or parties (provided that the benefit of the contract is assignable). Another exception is that under the Third Parties (Rights against Insurers) Act 1930, third parties can acquire rights against the insurer of an insolvent insured. There have been other exceptions, but those are beyond the scope of this book.

The Contracts (Rights of Third Parties) Act introduces a fundamental change to the privity of contract rule by providing that, in certain circumstances, a third party is entitled to enforce a contract to which he is not a party. The Act applies to England and Wales, and to Northern Ireland, but not to Scotland. This book only addresses the position under the law of England and Wales, and readers faced with a contract governed by the law of any other country should not assume that any of the legal issues addressed in this book will be the same under that other country's law.

The Act allows third parties to enforce a term of a contract in two situations. The first is where the contract expressly provides that the third party may enforce the term (which might seem obvious, but simply did not work in English law until now!). The second is where a contract is designed to confer some benefit on the third party (but does not expressly state that the third party may enforce that benefit) and on a proper construction of the contract it does not appear that the parties did not intend the term to be enforceable by the third party. (In other words, unless it seems that the third party is not meant to have rights, he does have rights.)

To be able to enforce the contractual term the third party must:

O   be expressly named in the contract; or

O   be identified as a member of a class of persons or meeting a parti-
      cular description. (Although, as at the time the contract is entered
      into, the third party need not be in existence – the type of situation
      that one can easily contemplate is a contract for the benefit of Super-
      market and any of its subsidiaries at any time. Those subsidiaries
      need not exist when the contract was made. Indeed, the class of
      people meeting the description of the bakeries would be relevant
      third parties.)

This new rule is likely to help in drawing up contracts under which the parties intend that a third party should be able to enforce a particular provision of a contract or even enforce the contract as a whole. For example:

O   a sale and purchase contract in respect of the shares or assets of a
      company where the buyer wishes to take the benefit of warranties
      (or promises given by the seller in relation to the shares or assets)
      for the benefit of itself and its assigns. A seller will often resist an
      attempt by the buyer to make the warranties assignable to a third
      party but, in the case where the seller does not object, the new rule
      will enable an assignee to obtain the benefit of a warranty by
      providing that the warranties are given for the benefit of the buyer
      and its assigns;

O   a sale and purchase contract of shares or assets where the seller
      enters into restrictive covenants (such as, not to compete with the
      business that it has just sold) and these restrictions are intended to
      be for the benefit of both the buyer named in the contract and other
      members of the buyers' group of companies; or

O   a software licence which is intended to benefit members of the same
      group as the licensee or where restrictions imposed on the licensee
      are intended to be enforceable by other members of the licensor's
      group or by a head licensor.

It seems clear from the wording in the Act that where a term purports to confer a benefit on a third party, there will be a rebuttable presumption that it was intended to be enforceable by the third party.

What this means is that whenever a contract refers to a third party, the person writing the contract needs to consider whether or not it is intended to confer an enforceable right on the third party. If this is intended, the contract should make it clear. Equally, if it is not intended, this should be made clear by expressly providing that the contract is not intended to confer an enforceable right on any (or, where appropriate, a particular) third party. Of course, most contracts are not drawn up so carefully, and so the presumption that the contract is intended to be enforceable by a third party, where that intention appears to be set out in the contract, will prevail and people who are clearly not actually party to a contract might find themselves in a position from which they can sue to enforce rights given to them under that contract.

The third party can, however, only enforce the relevant term in accordance with any other relevant terms of the contract. When enforcing the term he is entitled to the same remedies (such as damages, injunctions and specific performance and all the normal limitations on those remedies – see Chapter 8) as if he had been a party to the contract.

In the same way, the third party might be entitled to take advantage of an exclusion of limitation clause. This would, for example, enable Supplier, in its agreement with Supermarket, under which it is engaged to provide oven installation services, to Supermarket, to provide that Supermarket would have no right to claim against Supplier's employees for any act or omission of Supplier in performing the contract (with a view to Supplier's employees being able to rely on this exclusion clause).

The Act goes on to provide that, except in the certain limited circumstances referred to below, where a third party has a right to enforce a term of a contract, the parties to the contract cannot end the contract (or vary it so as to extinguish or alter the third party's right) without the third party's consent in three situations. These are:

O   where the third party has communicated his agreement to the relevant term to the party to the contract against whom it is enforceable (the 'promisor'); or

O   the promisor is aware that the third party has relied on the term; or

O   the promisor can reasonably be expected to have foreseen that the third party would rely on the term, and the third party has in fact relied on it.

The consent of the third party may be given by words, or by conduct or in writing, but if it is in writing and is sent by post or other means it is not treated as having been communicated to the promisor until it is received by the promisor (in other words, it is not deemed to be given when it is posted).

Where any of the circumstances just mentioned apply, the parties will only be able to end or vary the contract without the consent of the third party in the following circumstances:

O   if the contract contains an express term allowing it to be ended or varied without the consent of the third party; or

O   the contract provides that the consent of the third party is required

in the circumstances set out in the contract rather than in the circumstances set out in the Act; or

O   if a court or other tribunal dispenses with the third party's consent,
which it may do following an application by the parties to the
contract, and then only if that court or tribunal is satisfied that (1)
the third party's consent cannot be obtained because the third party
cannot be found or is mentally unable to give the third party's
consent, or (2) it cannot reasonably be ascertained whether or not
the third party has relied on the term in question. If the court or
tribunal does dispense with a third party's consent, it may impose
such conditions on the parties as it thinks fit, including a requirement
to pay compensation to the third party.

4

WHAT ARE THE KEY RELEVANT TERMS?

BACKGROUND

In Chapter 3 we looked at the issue of whether you are a party to the contract, and who the other party is (or parties are). Assuming that there is a contract to which you are a party, you need to consider the key relevant terms that might help you to get out of the contract. To fully understand your contract, you need to gather in the terms. And the first question that you need to get to the bottom of is this: is the contract made up of one document or several? To find the relevant terms, the relevant papers and information have to be collated. Before giving any advice as to the strength of your case, your lawyer will insist on collecting all the facts, and it will always be best to help speed along the legal process by keeping all correspondence and documents together, in date order, to pass to your lawyer. Careful notes should be taken of all meetings and telephone discussions, either during the meeting or phone call or as soon as possible after it takes place. In one celebrated case involving a famous entrepreneur and the UK's National Lottery, much was made of the contemporaneous notes taken by the entrepreneur during a visit to the toilet whilst discussions were ongoing! For ease of reference, printouts should be kept of all e-mails: both from you, and to you; you can rely on good electronic record-keeping, but a paper copy might still be the safer course.

The types of issue that we are going to be looking at in this chapter include these: what does the contract say about the duration of the contract? Is it still in force? Perhaps it can be ended by you at any time on giving notice irrespective of any breach by the other party. If the contract can be ended on notice, you must make sure that you follow the contract rules (if any). On giving notice – can it be given by hand, fax, post, e-mail? To whom should the notice be addressed and where? When is service to be deemed effective?

Those issues might sound quite straightforward, and in a well-drafted contract, which sets out all the terms, they will be. But, if we take the Garage Scenario, George might find this chapter will help him understand where he stands.

COLLECTING IN THE TERMS

Most contracts are not written down in a formal document, which remains unchanged over time. As has been seen in Chapter 2, most agreements are reached by a shake of hands, or in some other, informal, way. That is so, even with some large commercial agreements, and is very much the case in arrangements where the different parties are, at least at the time that they are entering into the contract, good friends.

To find out exactly what the contract's terms are, lawyers will be looking to see what evidence there is of the terms agreed. So, for example, when looking to see what the agreed price was, if it were not clear from a document which both parties could agree was a complete contractual statement of the terms, one would look to see, for example, what was invoiced and if that was paid. If one were looking to see what quantities, or other variables, were agreed, again, one might look at invoices, or bills of materials.

The reason why you might be trying to get out of the agreement is likely to be because the other party is not performing in the way you want, or because you simply no longer need services or goods of that kind, or you no longer want to be purchasing those goods or services from that provider, perhaps because you know you can get them cheaper elsewhere. In the Garage Scenario, George (or rather, his company, Rapid Repairs Limited) wants to get out of its contract because the contract is simply no longer the profitable proposition it had seemed to be when agreement was reached with Max (or rather, Rent-a-Car Limited).

Terms of the contract will most usefully be found in written documents. There are no formalities as to what written documents count, and what do not: so the back of an envelope is as good as finest quality parchment. All of the terms of the contract need to be found.

CONTRACT TERMS

To be able to ascertain exactly what the parties agreed to, the precise contract terms will need to be found. Even the simplest such exercise might not be as straightforward as it sounds – there is often doubt as to what a provision means, and the courts have developed a complex matrix of rules of construction and interpretation of contracts. Terms may be express (that is, actually stated) or implied (that is, not actually stated), and in this chapter, we are concerned with both types. Implied terms are, in essence, there to fill in the gaps, and so it is to express terms that one first must turn.

One might have thought that if there were a written contract, a party signing the document would be bound only by those terms. That is (generally) so, even if the signing party has not read them, and even if he or she does not understand their legal meaning. The issue, however, is that the fact that a contract has written terms does not mean that the signed document has all the contract terms. It certainly has a number of the express contract terms, but as has been seen in Chapter 2, contracts do not need to be in writing, and there is nothing to stop a contract being partly in writing and partly oral. Proving which oral statements are properly incorporated terms of the contract is one of the trickier parts of a lawyer's task.

BATTLE OF THE FORMS

It is very often the case that each party to a proposed agreement tries to insist that its standard terms of business apply. In the Bakery Scenario, Supplier issued a purchase order to Manufacturer with Supplier's standard terms and conditions of purchase on the reverse side. If Manufacturer had simply responded by sending an order confirmation letter, the contract terms would have been those included with Supplier's order.

Instead, Manufacturer responded by issuing Supplier with an invoice for the price, with Manufacturer's terms and conditions of sale on the reverse side.

This is known to lawyers as the 'battle of the forms', with each party seeking to make sure that its terms are those incorporated into the contract.

Who wins (by which we mean, whose standard terms of business end up as the contract terms)? The general rule is that the last party to put forward its terms before the contract is settled wins. If, here, Supplier made the down payment of £50 000 before the invoice was issued, it might be arguable that Supplier's terms had won, and that the contract was concluded before Manufacturer proposed its terms (on the back of the invoice). But each case has to be looked at on its own facts, and we have insufficient facts conclusively to determine the answer here. Generally, an invoice will prove to be too late to introduce terms.

One problem that often arises – parties fax the front side only of a double-sided document (such as the order form) to the other party, and unless the terms it is proposing are seen by the other party, it will almost invariably be the case that those terms do not apply. Placing orders by e-mail is equally likely to produce the result that terms are not sent through to the other party. That, essentially, raises the same issue as taking orders over the telephone:

making sure that staff are sufficiently trained to incorporate your terms into the contracts that your business is making can prove to be a key business issue.

IS IT A TERM?

In the build-up to the contract being made, many things will have been said by both parties. In the Bakery Scenario, Jim had managed to impress Bill with some technical jargon and industry knowledge and, later, had let Bill know that he had identified an oven that was likely to be suitable for Supermarket's needs. Other statements will have been made at various times, and it is unlikely that many of those statements will have been written down anywhere. In many regards, the replacing in business communications of telephone calls with e-mail notes improves things from the viewpoint of the party to whom promises are made, because if they are made, they will be made in writing that can be more readily found if a satisfactory e-mail policy is in place.

The next issue that needs to be addressed is that whereas some statements will have been intended to have contractual effect, others will have only been intended to be 'representations', or statements made to encourage the other person to enter into a contract, but not having the force of a contract term. If the statement is a contract term, its breach will entitle the other party to terminate the contract and claim damages. This issue is explored further in Chapter 6 but, for the purposes of this chapter, we need briefly to look at the issues a court will consider in determining if a statement is a representation or a contract term. The issues that a court is likely to have in mind when coming to its decision will include: how important is the truth of the statement? Was there a long or short time gap between the statement being made and the contract being agreed? Was the statement included in any of the written contract documents? The statement to a car dealer who bought a car from a private seller, that it was a 1948 model, was found not to be a contract term, even though the car was nine years older – this was a 1957 case, and the vintage model market that now exists did not yet exist. The seller 'honestly believed on reasonable grounds that the statement was true' (or so the court held in a 1965 case, involving a statement by a car dealer to a private buyer that a car had done 20 000 miles when in fact it had travelled some 100 000).

A contract term (or warranty, as it is sometimes called, by way of contrast to a representation), according to one of England's most senior judges of modern times, Lord Denning, is used 'in its ordinary English meaning to indicate a binding promise'.[1] In other words, to be a contract term, the ordinary English speaker would appreciate that the words used by the other party were intended to be taken as a promise of an action or state of events.

Straightforward? Well, not quite. It has long been accepted that there is no need for the promisor (the person making the promise) to use any special form of words to make clear that a promise is intended, but if no clear words to that effect are used, the courts must rely on the evidence surrounding the making of the promise, so that (as so often in contract law) the intention of the parties, based on their respective conduct, words and behaviour, rather than, say, unspoken thoughts, is what determines the matter. The questions already raised (how important? how long before the contract is made? was it written anywhere?) will all help the court decide the matter, but none of them, taken by itself, is capable of determining the answer. Let us examine some of these issues in a bit more depth. Remember, if you want to get out of an agreement, being able to prove that something is a contract term, which has been broken by the other party is going to be rather useful! In Chapter 6, we address the question of breach; here, the question of whether some statement is, or is not, a contract term is the issue. If a statement as to some aspect of the deal is clearly important to both sides to the contract, there is likely to be significant evidence to that effect, and in many commercial matters, that point is likely to have been put in writing. The difficult situation that more often arises is where the parties failed expressly to agree some key term – in one case, A stated that he would not want to know the price of B's goods if some fertilizing chemical had been used in growing them, and B then gave the price. The court decided that it was a term of the contract that the fertilizing chemical had not been used, because that was the only basis upon which A wanted to know the price.

In another case, the seller declared: 'you need not look for anything; the horse [this was a 1913 case] is perfectly sound', and then the seller went on, 'if there was anything the matter with the horse, I would tell you'. The court decided that the fact that the horse was 'perfectly sound' was a contract term – it was quite fair for the buyer to rely on the seller's promise. If the seller had used words such as 'as far as I know' or 'as far as I can tell', then it would not be fair to rely on the seller – he would have made clear, in plain English, that as far as he knew the thing was as he had set out, but sensible buyers would have had it checked out themselves.

The general rule (if there is one) would appear to be this: the more knowledgeable, or expert, one party is, the more likely it is that that party's statement as to the condition of the goods, or the requirement for services, or manner of their delivery, will be taken as having been a promise upon which the other party can rely. That proposition is best illustrated by the two cases involving the sale of cars already referred to in this chapter. In the first case, the seller was a private person, selling his car to a car dealer. The seller relied on the car's logbook to tell the age of the car. It turned out that the logbook was wrong; the car was older than the man had said it was. The court found that the statement as to the age of the car was not a contract term. In the second case, a car dealer made a false statement as to the mileage of a car he was selling to a consumer. That statement was held to be a contract term.

COLLATERAL CONTRACTS

Another area that must be considered when trying to collect in all the relevant contract terms is that which the courts have termed 'collateral contracts'. Here, the courts have sometimes been willing to address a statement which was intended to have contractual force as a separate, side contract (or collateral contract), collateral to the main contract. The situation is likely to involve one party stating that it will only contract if the other makes some specific promise about a specific thing – such as, not strictly to enforce a particular written term of the contract, or not to enforce it at all. In the case that has been mentioned already in this chapter, that of the goods on which the use of chemical fertilizers was a key issue, the courts could equally have found there to be a collateral contract to the effect that no such chemical fertilizer had been used, and the consideration (or buyer's promise in exchange) was that the buyer then agreed to the main purchase contract. Indeed, in a similar case, a prospective tenant made clear that he would only sign a lease if the landlord gave certain assurances about the drains being in a satisfactory state. The landlord gave those assurances, and the lease was then signed. When (as the reader might have predicted) the drains failed, the landlord was found liable under a collateral contract – but, no doubt, the court could equally have found that the landlord's drain promise was a contract term itself.

The last point on collateral contracts is this. English law has long held on to a rule called 'privity of contract'. What this means is that only those people who are parties to the contract can enforce it and be bound by it. It can be a harsh rule, and various devices have been built up by the courts over the years in an attempt to circumvent it. At the time of writing this book, an Act has recently completed its passing through Parliament, which, now it has become law, significantly varies the privity of contract rule, and makes the judicial circumvention devices less needed. That Act is addressed in Chapter 3 (see the section headed 'The Contracts (Rights of Third Parties) Act 1999'). One such device to circumvent that rule, however, is that of the collateral contract. In the main case on this point, the owners of the Shanklin Pier wanted their pier repainted. They contracted with painters, and required the painters to use Detel Products' paints, after Detel Products had promised the pier owners that the Detel paint would last for seven to ten years and was suitable for piers. Shanklin sued Detel when the paint proved unsuitable for piers only three months after it was used. Now Shanklin and Detel did not have a direct contract: the painters had bought the paint from Detel. The courts held that Shanklin could sue Detel, under a collateral contract, which the judges found to have terms which provided that if Detel specifies paint which painters were told to buy, Detel undertook the suitability of that paint for the job. Privity of contract is also further addressed in Chapter 3.

STANDARD TERMS

Another possible area in which to find written contract terms outside of what looks like the main (or only) contract document is where the contract document contains few (or no) terms itself, but refers one on to some other document that does. Examples occur everyday: bus and train tickets, for instance, always refer to 'standard conditions of carriage' (or the such like), which are intended to have contractual force. Do they?

When I buy my bus ticket, the contract is made by me asking for a fare from A to B; the driver or conductor tells me the price, I pay and I am handed the ticket. The contract is made. Do the terms apply to me? I do not usually read the ticket, but even if I do, it barely helps me, as it simply refers me on to some general conditions, probably not available to me to read on the bus journey. In order to be binding on me, a number of rules have evolved: the document must be of a type which a reasonable person would expect to set out (or otherwise include) contract terms – and examples from cases where this has been held to be the case include a train ticket and a receipt for the deposit of goods. On the other hand, a deckchair ticket and an automatic parking voucher have been held to be documents which a reasonable person would not assume to contain contract terms. Many of these situations have been addressed in old cases and, perhaps, today might be decided otherwise. The contract terms must be brought to the party's notice before or at the time the contract is made. Notice has been held by the courts to mean three things:

○   the person must know that there is writing on the document;
○   the person must know that the writing includes or refers to terms; and
○   the other person must do what is reasonably required to draw attention to the terms.

In addition, conditions of this kind will be contractual if there has been a 'course of dealing' between the parties and the parties have each let the other believe that the same terms that have applied between them until then would continue to apply, going forward.

SPOKEN TERMS

The final area in which the lawyer will look for expressly agreed terms of contracts are in spoken communication between the parties. So far, as should be clear, we have concentrated on written terms, or terms which have been expressly agreed and put in some written form. But what happens if there is a written agreement which appears to include all the provisions agreed by the parties, yet one of the parties asserts that there was some other term agreed, but which was not (for whatever reason) included in the written agreement? That other agreement might vary the written terms, add to them, remove them or flatly contradict them. Obviously convenience dictates that the certainty of written terms overrides the inconvenience of other, spoken, terms (and for many years, this was taken as sacrosanct). However, if some critical unwritten term were never given contractual force, great injustice could follow (although natural sympathy and prejudice, without reference to the particular facts of a case, might lead one to wonder why, if a term was so crucial, it was left unwritten). In fact, this spoken word rule also extends to documents which precede the final written agreement, such as correspondence, drafts of the final agreement and preliminary agreements (such as heads of terms or memoranda of understanding). The truth, however, is that the courts could not stomach a blunt rule that prevented a party from benefiting from some spoken promise by the other party (or, to look at it the other way round, which allowed a party to promise things when talking, but escape any liability for those promises if they were not put in writing). The current position of the law would seem to be that if enough evidence can be found to prove the existence of the oral promise, then there is no fundamental reason why that promise cannot be part of the contract.

Many written standard terms of business and many negotiated written contracts will include a clause headed 'entire agreement' or 'no other terms'. That type of clause is seeking to ensure that unless a term is included in the written document (or documents) identified as making up the whole of the contract, it does not count as a contract term. This type of clause is also seeking to ensure that statements made before the contract was finalized cannot be sued upon as being (mis)representations of fact. The general position today in relation to that type of clause is that the clause needs to be treated with a certain amount of caution – various Acts of Parliament and (in the consumer context) European Community laws have emasculated the effectiveness of entire agreements clauses. Nonetheless, if a clause is introduced into the draft of an agreement you should always ask yourself searching questions as to whether there have been any promises made or other statements made which ought to be included in the contract. In the same way that the law has increasingly moved to weaken the strength of an entire agreement clause, so it is not beyond possibility that the courts could move back somewhat from that approach and, in the right circumstances, decide to give some more life back to these clauses.

IMPLIED TERMS

As well as the express contract terms, the law (and specifically, the Sale of Goods Act 1979 and the Supply of Goods and Services Act 1982 (both as amended by the Sale and Supply of Goods Act 1994)) will imply certain terms into all contracts for the sale of goods and for the supply of services – again, there is much overlap between our discussion in this chapter and our discussion in Chapter 6, but for the purposes of this chapter it is especially important to remember that contracts (as was seen in Chapter 2) come in all shapes and sizes, in written and oral forms, and have express terms and implied ones.

Implied terms, like their express siblings, also come in many shapes and sizes and forms. Terms can be implied on the basis that the custom in a particular marketplace implies certain terms – the shipping, agriculture, metals and insurance worlds, all are mini-worlds, where contract terms are taken for granted and need not be negotiated. The fact that a particular market is highly developed or extremely basic does not matter – some of the most complex markets operate (at least in part) by custom, and so do some of the least developed ones. Terms can also be implied in fact or by law. For lawyers, a term is said to be implied in law if it is implied simply because the contract is of a certain type – in any sale of goods agreement, terms are implied by law that the seller can sell the goods, that the goods are of satisfactory quality and meet any description given to them. If the price of the goods has not been expressly agreed, the Sale of Goods Act provides that the buyer must pay a reasonable price for them (although what that price is remains an issue for the courts to decide). Terms are said to be implied by fact if, in a particular contract (irrespective of its type), the court can be convinced that the parties meant to include those terms. Terms will not readily be implied into a contract by the courts. The court will need to be convinced that the parties intended to include a particular term, but that is not the same thing as looking at a poorly constructed contract and getting the court to make it better. Lawyers have come up with various mechanisms for determining how the courts should go about implying terms. One test is to assess whether, without the clause, there is what has been termed 'business efficacy' in the contract – if that test is not met, then assuming people do not make bad contracts (that is, contracts which make no business sense to either party), terms can be implied to give the deal the efficacy that the parties must have intended. The other main test is that sometimes called the 'necessity' test (or, more helpfully, the 'officious bystander' test). This test requires the court to ask what the response of the parties would be to the officious bystander's suggestion that some clause be expressly included in the contract. If the parties' joint response were to be 'of course!', then that would be a firm indication that if that term was not expressly included in the contract, then it should be implied into it. The problem is that it remains undecided if the 'business efficacy' test is the same as, wider than or narrower than the 'officious bystander' test! For our purposes, it probably does not matter much; suffice it to say that terms can be implied by the courts, but they will only do so grudgingly and will not do so where the parties cannot be convinced to agree which version of the term is to be included – if that is what happens, the court cannot turn round and say 'of course!' to one or other version of a term.

The more detailed are the expressly agreed terms, the less likely will a court be to imply other terms – although it has also been argued (success-fully) that a largely incomplete, sparse written agreement was evidence of the fact that the parties had agreed a largely incomplete sparse agreement, and did not intend to fill any of the many gaps with implied terms.

In contrast to terms implied by fact, based on the particular factual matrix surrounding a contract, terms are implied by law into all contracts that meet certain objective criteria – such as, as has been stated already, that the contract is a contract for the sale of goods. In the case of a term implied by law, the parties' unstated intention is irrelevant – if one sells goods and the other buys them, terms are implied into that transaction, unless the parties expressly agree that those terms will not be implied. If an express term does exclude the implication of a term at law, other laws (particularly the Unfair Contract Terms Act 1977) might actually override that express agreement (but, again, that is an area beyond the scope of this book, and can be found addressed in any number of contract law textbooks).

So, having discovered where and what the contract terms are, the next task is to seek to discover what they mean. Like many of the issues raised in this chapter, some aspects of the construction of the contract's terms are left for Chapter 6.

ENDING THE CONTRACT

Over three chapters into this book, it is time to ask our main question: how can you get out of your agreement? There are various possible scenarios:

1   The contract term comes to an end at a pre-agreed time (usually the time that the parties agreed it would end when they agreed the contract in the first place).

2   Either party is entitled under the terms of the contract to end the contract by giving notice.

3   The parties agree to it ending.

4   There are what lawyers call (with no sense of irony) 'frustration' or other events outside the parties' control which result in the contract

coming to an end or which allow one (or both) of the parties to get out of their agreement.

5   Competition law helps you to escape from the objectionable terms – this is addressed in Chapter 5.

6   One party breaks its obligations under the contract and the other party ends it – this is the subject matter of Chapter 6.

7   You walk away from the contract – and the consequences of that are dealt with in Chapter 8.

In this chapter, we are looking at possibilities (1) to (4).

CONTRACT TERM COMES TO AN END

Although this might seem the most straightforward and likely method of bringing a contract to an end – it simply expires at the end of an agreed term – it does not always give either party the certainty they are both looking for. Let us see why that might be so.

Because proving what the terms of the contract mean is so important, we will spend some time here looking, in outline, at the rules used by the courts to determine what the parties intended by their agreement. The goal of the exercise is to discover what the parties meant when they reached their agreement, and for this section our concern is to work out when the contract term was meant to run out.

The most important rule of contract construction is that the parties must have intended what they said, and 'intention' in this sense is probably closest to 'what is the meaning of the words', rather than 'what did the parties mean to say'. The first of those phrases looks at the words actually used, whereas the second is, in effect, starting from a presumption that the words are unclear and the parties meant to use others! Of course, by interpreting 'intention' as 'meaning', apparent injustices can follow – if the parties meant to say one thing, but the meaning of the words used is something else, the courts should, nonetheless, give the words their common meaning. There is a perfectly good reason for the courts to have adopted this rule – if, as we saw in Chapter 3, you are now party to a contract, but you were not the original contracting party, it is only fair that you are bound by what the words mean, and not by what the original contracting parties meant them to mean. If you were to be bound by what the original contracting parties meant their words to mean, you would need to arrange what would end up amounting to a trial, where each party would be cross-examined as to what it meant each word of the contract to mean – and that would both put an end to any fluidity in the world of contracts and add a level of uncertainty that cannot possibly be sustained.

Increasingly, however, courts have leant towards ascertaining the parties' intentions from the language used, but in light of the surrounding circum-stances – in other words, attention has shifted towards the commercial purpose of the contract, based on the judge's years of experience of contracts of the particular type, although where the words used in a contract are clear, the court must give them their clear meaning even if there is no obvious commercial benefit in giving them that clear meaning.

So, all very well, but how do you know when the contract has come to an end?

When does the contract come to an end?

There have been many cases addressing what, on the face of it, appears to be some very straightforward language. If we suppose that I have contracted to provide services 'until 1 September 2004', when does my obligation end? Does it end at midnight at the end of 31 August 2004? Or at midnight on 1 September 2004? Or at close of business on 1 September 2004 – and is that 5 p.m., 5.30 p.m. or 6 p.m.? The courts, rather unhelpfully, have only been able to find that the words 'until' and 'till' are ambiguous – they can be inclusive or exclusive, and their actual meaning will depend on the context and the subject matter of the contract. A footballer contracted 'until the end of the match' knows that the match ends when the referee finally blows the whistle, but if the footballer is contracted 'until the end of the season' that might not give the same, absolute certainty.

The word 'from' has been found to be equally unclear. Again, if I contract to provide services for 'three years from 1 January 2001', is 1 January 2004 included or excluded? The general rule is that the 'from' date itself is to be excluded – although, on the facts, the general rule should only be seen as a starting presumption, and not definitive in any sense. So, what does paragraph 2 of Max's letter in the Garage Scenario mean?

Other commonly seen words, such as 'on' and 'upon', have been variously found by the courts to mean 'before', 'at the same time as', or 'after' a given thing happening!

Time itself has been interpreted by courts in many cases. The word 'year' may mean a calendar year (that is, from, and including, 1 January to, and including 31 December) or a 12-month period calculated from any other date (and in one case, where an employee had started work on 13 October in one year and ended 365 days later on 11 October in the next year – which was a leap year – his service was found not to have been for a year, even though he had served for 365 days). In some industries, a 'year' has a very specific meaning, so in the case of an actress engaged for 'three years', the court held that to mean 'three theatrical seasons' – leaving her, properly, unpaid for parts of the 36 months. In the Garage Scenario a 'year' (as used in paragraph 6 of Max's letter) probably means a 12-month period – although when that runs from is unclear from the facts set out in Chapter 1.

Often, contracts refer to 'quarters' or 'quarter days', which are usually taken to refer to the traditional quarter days of 25 March, 24 June, 29 September and 25 December, but a 'quarter' (where used as part of a year) can mean any three-month period, depending on the circumstances. At least paragraph 6 of Max's letter is quite clear in that regard.

A 'month' will generally mean a calendar month (that is, January, February, and so on) rather than a 28-, 29-, 30- or 31-day period.

If a contract starts, however, on say 18 March, and is said to run for six months, the courts have applied the 'corresponding date rule', which means that it expires on the day of the month bearing the same number as the date on which the period begins (namely 18 September) or, if there is no such corresponding day (six months from 31 May would fall on the non-existent 31 November), on the last day of the month (so, in that case, 30 November).

'Day' can mean a calendar day (Monday, Tuesday, and so on) or a 24-hour period, depending on the circumstances, and a 'working day' normally means a day which is not a holiday, and can sometimes be narrowed down to the period (such as 9 a.m. to 5 p.m.) when people are actually working.

Even if you are confident that the contract does come to an end at a given time, there is a risk that it might continue in force, if the parties continue to operate under its terms. This is one example of the situation which requires the party to give 'reasonable' notice of actual termination. What is reasonable in a two-year term contract might not be the same as what is reasonable in a five-year contract, and, below, some guidance from decided cases is set out. That might not be a commercial problem if both parties want to continue the contract, but if only one of them does, then the contract will not continue. At that point, either the customer is left without the service, or the supplier is left without a customer, but with its overheads.

In the Garage Scenario, Max's letter clearly states that the agreement would commence 'today' (whenever that was), and 'continue for five years …'. If we accept for these purposes that that letter does, indeed, set out all of the relevant contract terms, then we cannot take forward the possibility that the contract is terminable on reasonable notice. But if we are wrong, or if the second paragraph of Max's letter had not been written, and we were faced with an open-ended contract for the provision of services, or the sale or supply of goods, that contract might be capable of being ended on reasonable notice. The general rule nowadays would appear to be that an agreement which is silent as to when and how it is to end will only be capable of being ended if the circumstances support a finding that the parties intended (and, here, the word must mean 'meant') it to be capable of being ended. All that can be said here is that if the contract can be ended, but the contract itself makes no provision for how long the notice period is to be, the courts will decide on how long 'reasonable notice' is in each particular case.

There is, however, a recent case that ought to keep parties (and their lawyers) awake at night: in *Harbinger* v. *GE Information Services*,[2] the contract was for Harbinger to provide support and maintenance to GE Information Services 'in perpetuity'. The Court of Appeal decided that 'in perpetuity' meant precisely that – the obligation was to continue without limit in time, so that the service provider could not terminate the obligation (even if, as the original High Court judge had held, this flouted business common sense)! However, on the basis of the particular contract, once the supported technology had been superseded, the customer would stop paying annual support fees and the service obligation would end. Nonetheless, the ramifications of this decision could be far-reaching.

A number of cases will help illustrate the point made here.

Example 1 *Prosperity Ltd* v. *Lloyds Bank*.[3] A bank gave its customer one month's notice before closing its account. Its customer, an insurance company, required its policyholders to pay premiums into the bank account, and the court decided that one month's notice was not reasonable in those circumstances.

Example 2 *Kores Manufacturing Co. Ltd* v. *Kolok Manufacturing Co. Ltd*.[4] An agreement between the parties not to employ anyone who had been an employee of the other during the previous five years was held to be terminable on twelve months' notice.

Bauman v. *Hulton Press Ltd*.[5] An employment contract which had run for some three years was found to be terminable only after reasonable notice was given, and six months was a reasonable period of notice. In *Orman* v. *Saville Sportswear Ltd*,[6] another case, seven days' notice given to terminate the employment contract was insufficient notice.

Example 3 *Milner & Son* v. *Bilton (Percy) Ltd*.[7] A solicitor's retainer to provide legal services in respect of a building development was found to be terminable on reasonable notice (although what that was was unstated). On the other hand, *Gore District Council* v. *Power Co. Ltd*,[8] an electricity board agreed to supply the local authority electricity at a fixed price 'for all time hereafter' and it could not terminate its agreement, even by giving reasonable notice.

In the next section but one, we consider those contracts where the parties have agreed that notice can be given to exit.

THE CONTRACT ENDS BECAUSE IT HAS BEEN PERFORMED

A contract can come to an end, because both parties have done what they agreed to do – when I buy my bus ticket, the bus company agrees to take me to my destination. When I get off the bus, our contract is said to be discharged – it no longer binds us.

ENDING THE CONTRACT BY GIVING NOTICE

Many contracts will have clauses which provide that at the end of a fixed term, the contract rolls on until terminated by either party giving the other a stated period of notice. In that case, you need to read the clause carefully to see:

O   when can notice be given?
O   when can the notice period expire (and termination become effective)?

Note that what we are addressing here is not getting out of a contract because the other party is in breach of its obligations but simply using a power included within the contract to end it. Note also that terminating a contract by using an agreed notice provision does not (necessarily) stop you also from claiming damages from the other party for a breach of contract.

Clause wording to look for

The type of contract term one would often see would be some variation on one of the following two terms:

1   'Notice may be given at any time [on or] after the end of the [Fixed] Term.'
2   'Notice is to be effective at any time [on or] after the end of the [Fixed] Term.'

If the notice period is six months, Clause (1) allows you to get out of the contract six months earlier than Clause (1). Clause (1) says that notice can only be given after, say, 31 December 2001 and, therefore, will only be effective on or after 30 June 2002. Clause (2), on the other hand, says that notice can be given at any time on or after 30 June 2002, and will, therefore, be effective on or after 31 December 2002 – a difference of six months. In the Garage Scenario, Max's letter proposed the following: that the agreement 'will continue for five years after which either of us can end it on 90 days' notice'. That is a Clause (1) type clause.

Can either party give the notice?

It is not uncommon to agree that if the Supplier can give notice, it must give a longer notice period than the Customer. The reason for this is that the Customer will have to find another supplier and negotiate a new contract. That will take time. On the other hand, the Supplier is likely to have built in some cost element to its fee to the Customer to cover it for its possible excess capacity (or underemployment of assets) on termination.

Most contracts, in fact, do not distinguish between the notice period to be given by the Customer and that to be given by the Supplier; in negotiating the terms of the contract, one party is rarely in a sufficiently strong negotiating position to obtain an advantage when it comes to giving notice to get out of the contract.

TERMINATION 'AT WILL' OR 'FOR CONVENIENCE'

By customer

Some contracts include provisions allowing one of the parties (and if not both, the party with the stronger bargaining position at the time the contract was agreed, will be the more likely one to have this right) to terminate 'for convenience' or 'at will' whenever it decides (usually on three or six months' notice) and usually so as to terminate on an anniversary date.

The financial consequences of agreeing this would typically be that if the Customer does terminate for convenience, it pays the Supplier some form of early termination compensation (estimated by reference to the loss to the Supplier of its otherwise achievable future income from the contract, and discounted to reflect how far down the contract the parties are at termination and the Supplier's ability to replace the Customer's contract with other business).

In some sectors where shorter-term contracts are the norm, it is less likely that compensation will be payable. But in longer-term sectors, such as, for example, pensions administration, where five-year terms are more common and the handover and start-up costs are high (for both parties), this is likely to generate considerable discussion at contract negotiation stage.

By supplier

It is not unknown (but far less common) for Suppliers also to have such rights. In this case, the Customer needs to be protected to the extent necessary to enable it to be assured of service continuity, and transitional or exit services become very important.

In negotiating that type of provision, the Customer will need to consider what level of compensation it needs; the extra costs that might be incurred by the Customer could include the costs of:

1   Retendering
2   Interviewing/assessing suppliers
3   Drawing up the replacement contract
4   Negotiating the replacement contract
5   Asset replacement/transfer.

It is not possible to quantify the extent of such costs and the costs highlighted should be seen as guidelines for management to build upon. In management time costs alone, stages (1) to (4) could each take up between one and three months.

In addition, there are bound to be various non-financial costs, for example, of staff unrest, lack of continuity of service and inconvenience.

OTHER EVENTS ENTITLING TERMINATION

In Chapters 5 and 6, various events are discussed which might entitle one party to terminate the agreement. This chapter highlights other routes out of the contract.

Perhaps a startling fact, but it is quite common to find termination provisions in clauses not headed 'termination'. The two most usual clauses containing rights to terminate are 'force majeure' clauses and 'severance' clauses. In addition, the law has developed a concept called 'frustration'.

'Force majeure' is a term which, essentially, means an act beyond the party's control; types of things likely to be included are floods, wars or strikes. Despite the phrase being used in many contracts, it does not have an exact legal meaning and the phrase 'the usual force majeure clauses to apply' was held to be too unclear to be enforceable. Accordingly, if included in a contract, it needs to be defined.

Force majeure clauses will sometimes provide that if the event outside the Supplier's control continues for, say, 60 days, so that the Supplier is unable to provide the services, the Customer may terminate.

Severance clauses will often state that if the fundamental core of the contract is severed (for whatever reason), the contract may be terminated. The usual type of severance clause aims to provide that if some part of the contract is unenforceable (because, for example, it is illegal or against public policy), but other parts would be enforceable if they could stand alone, then the enforceable parts should be enforceable and the unenforceable parts severed.

The courts have adopted two general rules on severance clauses: the court will not rewrite the contract, and the court will not sever the unenforceable parts unless that is in accordance with public policy. So, a contract whose main purpose was to defraud the Inland Revenue was held to be one which could not benefit from a severance clause.

Severance clauses are usually drafted in two parts – the first asks the court to strike out any offending provisions of the contract and to enforce the remainder; the second part allows either party to terminate the contract if its fundamental purpose is so emasculated that there is no commercial point in proceeding (or, to put the horse before the cart, if, had the parties known that all that would be in their contract were the remaining clauses, they would not have entered into it in the first place).

The other way that a contract might be ended without agreement of the parties and in circumstances where neither party is in breach is under the rule known as 'frustration'.

Frustration allows a contract to be ended if something happens after the contract is made, which makes it physically or commercially impossible for the contract to be performed or which makes the obligations totally different from that which the parties agreed. The concept of 'frustration' is narrow and the courts will try not to use it, as there is a concern that parties should take the rough with the smooth, and not be able to claim frustration when they find themselves on a roundabout rather than a swing. In any event, the use of a force majeure clause significantly reduces the scope for frustration to be raised as an argument – the very event which appears to frustrate the contract, if outside the party's control, will be a force majeure event, suspending the obligation to perform rather than destroying the purpose of the contract.

The most famous event of frustration was the cancellation of Edward VII's coronation procession in 1902, because of the king's illness. In one case, the defendant agreed to hire rooms in the claimant's central London building to look out over the procession due to pass by through the streets below. Although the contract did not mention the procession, the parties did not dispute that the only purpose for the hiring was to watch the procession. There was no point in the rooms' owner bothering to argue otherwise: people simply do not hire rooms to overlook any old street for a few hours! On learning of the cancellation, the defendant refused to pay the agreed rent, and the Court of Appeal agreed, on the grounds that the 'procession was the foundation of this contract and that the non-happening of it prevented the performance of the contract'. There was no issue that the room and its windows were exactly what the defendant had ordered, and the address had not changed.

Other examples of frustrating events include, unsurprisingly, the death of the person contracted to provide personal services, and, under Section 7 of the Sale of Goods Act 1979, where there is a contract to sell specific goods and (without fault of the buyer or seller) those goods perish before risk passes to the buyer.

'ENTITLED TO TERMINATE'

The negotiators charged with getting the contract agreed should also understand how the language used in the termination clauses affects their respective rights.

If the Customer is 'entitled to' or 'may' terminate, it does not have to terminate. It might not want to terminate. It might be better off recovering damages from the Supplier and staying with the Supplier.

If the clause provides that 'the contract shall terminate if . . . ', the parties (in the absence of agreement at the time to the contrary) have no option: the contract falls away with all the concomitant consequences.

So those are some of the ways in which contracts might allow a get out. But many contracts set out very precise procedures for giving notices – including termination notices. A failure to give notice in the correct, contractually agreed, way could easily result in the contract not being terminated at all.

HOW IS NOTICE TO BE GIVEN?

In order to be effective, notice of termination has to be given strictly in accordance with the terms of the contract.

This is a standard form of notice provision which can be found (in this, or very similar, form – perhaps a little shorter, sometimes a bit longer) in many commercial agreements:

1. **Notices**

1.1 Any notice under or in connection with this Agreement shall be in writing and shall be delivered by hand, or sent by first class post (or by airmail if sent abroad) or by fax as follows:

1.1.1 if to Party A to:
Address:
Fax No:
Marked for the attention of:

1.1.2 if to Party B to:
Address:
Fax No:
Marked for the attention of:

or to such other person, address or fax number as either party may specify to the other from time to time by notice given in accordance with this Agreement provided that any party giving any notice by fax shall also send a copy of that notice by post, which shall be placed in the post by that party on the date of transmission of the fax or the next Working Day thereafter.

2.2 In the absence of evidence of earlier receipt, any properly addressed notice shall be deemed to have been duly given:

2.2.1 if sent by first class post, [two] Working Days after posting, provided that there are no postal strikes affecting the relevant areas;

2.2.2 if sent by airmail, seven days after posting, provided that there are no postal strikes affecting the relevant areas;

2.2.3 if sent by fax, on completion of its transmission (if
during the Normal Working Hours of the
recipient) or at 10 a.m. on the next Working Day
(if any part of the fax was transmitted outside the
recipient's Normal Working Hours).

Note the very carefully worded requirements of this clause: the form in which it may be served, to whom it must be addressed, when it is deemed served – although the post service might be faster than this clause provides, there is no point in having to pay lawyers to argue over when the notice was served, and the clause therefore deems when the notice was served if the receiving party denies having received the notice sooner, or, indeed, at all. This is often crucial as it is often the case that termination can only occur on the anniversary of the contract date and at least 90 days' notice of termination is required: if the notice is not deemed served on a given day, the termination might not be effective and the agreement will continue in force for a whole year (or, in many cases, where a contract is written so that it rolls on for two, three or more years, for a whole two, three or more years) longer than the party serving the notice intended it to do. Note also that once our advice of termination has been properly and validly given, it can only be withdrawn if the other party agrees to its withdrawal.

TERMINATION BY AGREEMENT

We have seen, in Chapter 2, the four key requirements for any contract to have legal effect. Offer, acceptance, consideration and intention to create legal relations are also the four key requirements of an agreement that ends the contract.

In agreeing to terminate the contract, it is usually rather easy to find three of the four key requirements – offer ('shall we end this contract?'), acceptance ('yes!') and intention to create legal relations. Finding consideration in some situations is harder.

Where each party still has obligations to perform, each can promise to allow the other not to have to perform its obligations (or, to give that its formal due, each can discharge the other from further performance), and that mutuality of promises (or discharges) is enough consideration for the agreement to end the existing agreement.

Where only one party has obligations still to perform, allowing it off the hook of further performance goes one way only, and so finding consideration is harder. The easiest way to overcome that problem is to package the termination agreement as a deed which (as was explained in Chapter 2) does away with the need for mutual promises as consideration.

The other, and perhaps most common way that agreement is reached to end a contract is by way of a compromise agreement where things have gone wrong in the original agreement, and the parties agree to go their separate ways apart, say, from the supplier agreeing to help effect a smooth handover to the new supplier and the customer agreeing to pay something for that support. The disadvantage of this type of compromise is that it is not a clean break, although it will usually reserve the customer's right to sue for damages resulting from the underlying breach. The question of compromises is more fully addressed in Chapter 9.

One final thing to note here is that although it helps (in terms of clarity) if the agreement ending the original agreement uses a term like 'rescind', 'abandon', 'discharge' or (in plain English) 'end', there is no need for that type of language.

Now, in the ideal world, all agreements are expressly agreed and documented; of course, in the real world, not all agreements are. Agreements can be terminated by the implied agreement of the parties, although unless there is an intention to completely extinguish the main agreement, the failure clearly and unambiguously to declare the main agreement at an end could be read by a judge as being a variation of its terms, rather than its termination.

One way that parties can find that their agreement is over by implication is if they enter into a further contract with each other which is inconsistent with their first agreement. Even though their second agreement might fail even to mention their first, if it is not possible to read it in any way other than as being inconsistent with an intention that the first agreement survive, then the first agreement ends. Of course, as has been stated elsewhere in this chapter, the second agreement must satisfy the requirements of any contract (offer, acceptance, consideration and intention to create legal relations). If it is either not possible to understand or perform the second contract without the first still being in place, the second will not end the first, but vary it.

The second, implied, way of ending an agreement is where the parties behave in such a way that the contract is considered at an end. If one of the parties says or does something in such a way that the other can reasonably rely on that statement or act as meaning that the contract is over, the sayer or doer cannot then argue that the contract is still alive. Action, in this situation, can include inaction: if one party fails to perform its side of the deal for a very long time, it might be reasonable for the other party to consider that it had no intention ever to perform, and so treat the contract as ended. This type of situation is one which even the most senior judges have always found to be rather tricky, and no reader of this book should rush ahead, treating his or her contract as over, simply because of, say, the other party's delay.

NOTES

1   *Oscar Chess* v. *Williams* [1957] 1 WLR 370, at 374.
2   *Harbinger* v. *GE Information Services* [2000] 1 All ER (Comm.) 166.

3   *Prosperity Ltd* v. *Lloyds Bank* (1923) 39 TLR 372 (KB Div.).

4   *Kores Manufacturing Co. Ltd* v. *Kolok Manufacturing Co. Ltd* [1958]
        2 WLR 858.

5   *Bauman* v. *Hulton Press Ltd* [1952] 1 All ER 1121.

6   *Orman* v. *Saville Sportswear Ltd* [1960] 1 WLR 1055.

7   *Milner & Son* v. *Bilton (Percy) Ltd* [1966] 1 WLR 1582.

8   *Gore District Council* v. *Power Co. Ltd* [1996] 1 NZLR 58.

5

COMPETITION LAW ISSUES

PART I: INTRODUCTION

Hundreds of commercial contracts contain clauses which are not worth the paper they are written on. Why? Because those agreements do not comply with competition laws, so vital parts of them will not be enforceable.

If you are trying to get out of an agreement, you may be able to use this to your advantage. Suppose your agreement with your supplier prevents you getting supplies from anyone else. If that obligation turns out to be unenforceable, you will be free to buy elsewhere.

Sometimes, competition law can get you out of unwanted commitments: but it can cut both ways, by getting others out of their unwanted commitments to you. Competition law may not be top of your agenda when considering how to get out of an agreement, but you should not ignore it. Competition law is a highly technical area and this chapter is not intended to cover every possible aspect of it, but to outline when the competition laws may be relevant.

Both UK and European competition laws may be relevant. Several questions need to be answered to identify which (if any) competition laws may affect your agreement. The most important questions are:

1   When was the agreement made?
2   Where is trade affected by the agreement – in the UK and/or within Europe?
3   Does the agreement prevent, restrict or distort competition?
4   Is another party to the agreement in a dominant position on the relevant market?
5   Does the agreement represent an abuse of that dominant position?

6   Is the agreement excluded or exempt from relevant competition law?
7   Has the agreement been approved by the relevant authorities?

The importance of the date of your agreement is that it affects which UK competition law(s) can apply to it. If it was made before 9 November 1998, then the Restrictive Trade Practices Act 1976 (RTPA) may be relevant; the Resale Prices Act 1976 and the Competition Act 1998 may also be relevant. If it was made after 1 March 2000, then the Competition Act 1998 will apply; the position is more complicated for agreements made between those two dates.

Where the agreement affects trade will determine whether UK and/or EU competition law applies to it. If the agreement has an effect (even a potential effect) on trade between European Union (EU) member states[1] – such as an agreement by Fiat to supply cars made in Italy to a British dealer – then European competition law (Articles 81 and 82 of the Treaty of Rome[2]) will be relevant. If it only affects trade in all or part of the UK, then only UK competition law can be relevant.

PART II: UK LAW

(A) AGREEMENTS MADE BEFORE 1 MARCH 2000

If your agreement was made before 1 March 2000, you need to consider the legislation which existed before the Competition Act 1998, especially the RTPA. This still affects agreements made before 1 March 2000, especially those made before 9 November 1998, when the Competition Act 1998 was enacted. This means that the RTPA may still enable one party to an agreement to get out of it: or, at least, to escape from some of its terms.

If your agreement was made on or after 1 March 2000, you do not need to worry about these old laws, and you can go on to B below.

1 The RTPA

1.1 Introduction The RTPA required details of certain agreements to be given to the Office of Fair Trading (OFT) within a specified time limit (usually three months after the agreement was made). There are three important consequences if those details were not given to the OFT on time:

O   'relevant restrictions' contained in the agreement are unenforceable (the term 'relevant restriction' is explained below);
O   it is unlawful for any party to the agreement to operate or try to enforce those restrictions; and
O   affected third parties can also claim damages from anyone who gives effect to the restrictions.

In terms of getting out of an agreement, it is the first of these which is most important. If details of your agreement should have been given to the OFT, but they were not, the relevant restrictions on you in that agreement will be unenforceable. This could be good news if you wish to get out of that agreement – or, at least, to be free from those restrictions.

The RTPA was extremely technical. It looked at the form of agreements, not their economic effect. Agreements which were caught were said to be 'registrable', because they were subject to registration.

1.2 Examples In 1989, a milkman (Mr Baines) signed an agreement with a dairy (Associated Dairies). It required him to buy all his milk from the dairy and not to retail milk to the dairy's customers. The dairy was forbidden to sell milk to his customers. Details of the agreement were not given to the OFT. Mr Baines began buying milk from another supplier. The dairy went to court to stop him doing so. The milkman claimed his obligation to buy milk only from the dairy was unenforceable, because details of the agreement had not been given to the OFT. The Court of Appeal agreed with him, and found him able to escape the express prohibition in his agreement; but the House of Lords did not, and found that his agreement remained in place.[3]

In 1977, Topliss Showers Ltd and Gessey & Son Ltd entered into a settlement agreement, following disputes between them. Details of the agreement were not provided to the OFT. Topliss Showers claimed damages against Gessey & Son for alleged breaches of the settlement agreement. Gessey & Son argued that the restrictions in the settlement agreement were registrable under the RTPA and because it had not been registered, it was unenforceable. The judge agreed, even though he did so 'without enthusiasm because it seems to me to be a very technical and artificial defence'.[4]

So, in an appropriate case, the RTPA could free you from the very restriction which is giving you most grief.

1.3 What made an agreement registrable? There were three basic requirements for an agreement to be registrable. First, there had to be an agreement (which did not have to be in writing, or legally binding). Second, the agreement had to be between at least two parties who carried on business in the UK in the supply of goods (or two doing so in the supply of services) because goods and services were treated separately. Finally, at least two parties had to accept 'relevant restrictions' under that agreement. The parties who accepted restrictions did not have to be the same as those who carried on business in the UK.

Agreements which formed part of the same transaction (such as a supply agreement which was part of a joint venture) were treated as one 'arrangement' and considered as a whole, not separately, to see if they were registrable under the RTPA.

Connected companies (such as a parent company and its subsidiaries) counted as one 'party' for the purpose of the RTPA. So did individuals who were partners in a business partnership.

1.4 Relevant restrictions Not every restriction on a party's behaviour was relevant to the RTPA. Only those restrictions listed in the RTPA were relevant. The most important types of relevant restrictions concerned:

O   the prices to be charged or paid – for example, if two supermarkets each agreed not to charge less than 25p for a can of baked beans;

O   the terms or conditions on which goods or services are to be supplied – for example, if a holiday company agreed with its bankers not to accept holiday bookings unless customers paid a 50 per cent deposit;

O   the quantities or descriptions of goods to be produced, supplied or acquired – for example, if a brewery agreed not to produce more than 500 000 barrels a year of its best bitter;

O   the people with whom business is to be done. This caught exclusivity requirements: for example, if a component supplier agreed not to supply components to any car manufacturer besides its largest customer; and

O   the areas or places where business is to be done – for example, if McDonald's agreed with a franchisee not to open another McDonald's restaurant within half a mile of the franchisee's restaurant.

A 'restriction' did not have to be absolute, but had to limit an existing freedom. Restrictions relating to the goods or services to be supplied under the agreement were generally disregarded.

So, if you are considering whether the RTPA might help you get out of an agreement made before 1 March 2000, watch out for relevant restrictions, such as:

O   clauses giving exclusive rights – for example, in a supply agreement;

O   non-compete covenants – such as a clause preventing the seller of a company from carrying on a competing business after the sale;

O   any allocation of customers or markets – for example, an agreement between two rival building companies to share out tenders for building contracts between them; or

O   any controls on business with third parties – such as what business can be done or what prices can be charged.

If the agreement contains a relevant restriction on you, see if you can find a relevant restriction on the other party. Even a minor one might be enough for the agreement to be caught.

We acted for a company which had a concession in a department store. There were several obvious restrictions on our client in the agreement. Our client wanted to get out of some of them. Fortunately, the store had agreed to give staff discounts to our client's employees. This was a restriction on their freedom to set prices. This relevant restriction, plus those on our client, was enough to make the agreement registrable, because at least two parties must accept relevant restrictions. The store had not taken the point and so had not given details of the agreement to the OFT. This would have freed our client from the restrictions on it, but in the end the matter was settled without the point having to be taken.

1.5 Registration Details of registrable and notifiable agreements had to be given to the OFT within three months of the date of the agreement. Any party to an agreement could provide details of it to the OFT. Once the OFT received the agreement, they decided whether the agreement was registrable. If it was, it was placed on a public register, but some confidential parts of it could be kept private. You can therefore search the public register to see if your agreement was registered.

1.6 The dilution of the RTPA The RTPA was repealed on 1 March 2000. For several years before then, its impact was progressively diluted as more and more agreements were treated as 'non-notifiable', or exempted from its provisions. (Essentially, between 1989 and 1998 agreements containing certain restrictions, or which were of certain types, or which were made between parties with low enough turnover, became non-notifiable.) The newer the agreement, the less likely it is to have been 'caught' by the RTPA, so the less likely it is that you can rely on the RTPA to try to get out of key parts of the agreement. This is why the date of the agreement is so important.

1.7 Changes in circumstances Changes in circumstances could make an agreement registrable, for example, a change in the activities or status of the parties. If, for example, one party to an agreement did not carry on business in the UK when the agreement was made, but started to do so a year later, this may make an agreement registrable – because an agreement could only be registrable if two or more of the parties to it carried on business in the UK in the supply of goods, or two or more did so in the supply of services.

So, if you are considering whether the RTPA could help you get out of an agreement (or key parts of it), you and your lawyer need not only to consider when the agreement was made, but also what has changed since then. You may also need to consider the parties' turnover, depending on when the agreement was made.

1.8 Summary Remember the RTPA for agreements made before 1 March 2000 – it could help you get out of some unwanted obligations, just like Gessey & Son did. If you want to get out of an agreement made before 1

March 2000, have it checked by a specialist lawyer to see if it was registrable and notifiable under the RTPA – and if so, whether details of it were given to the OFT.

If details of the agreement should have been given to the OFT, but were not given to the OFT on time (or at all), then the other party will not be able to make you perform the relevant restrictions on you in that agreement. But this cuts both ways, so you will not be able to enforce relevant restrictions against the other party.

If the restrictions on you are more important, it may well be worth relying on the RTPA to try to get out of your agreement.

2 Resale Prices Act 1976

2.1 If your agreement was made before 1 March 2000, you also need to consider the Resale Prices Act 1976 (RPA). This made it unlawful for manufacturers or suppliers to impose or enforce a minimum price at which their goods could be resold by dealers or retailers, unless those goods had been exempted.

2.2 The RPA made agreements between suppliers and dealers to establish minimum prices void – so a requirement that a dealer must charge minimum prices could not lawfully be included in an agreement, or enforced. If Giant Garages' agreement with its vehicle supplier, Megacars, said that Giant Garages would not charge less than £10 000 for any new Megacar vehicle supplied by Megacar, that clause could not be enforced against Giant Garages by Megacars.

2.3 Agreements between dealers and suppliers could, however, include recommended prices. The RPA did not prevent agreements specifying a maximum price at which a dealer could sell the product.

2.4 The RPA was also repealed by the Competition Act, with effect from 1 March 2000. But the Competition Act continues the RPA's hostility to controlling resale prices.

(B) COMPETITION ACT 1998

1 Introduction

If your agreement affects trade in any part of the UK, then the Competition Act 1998 may be relevant to it. (If your agreement was made on or after 1 March 2000, then you will not need to consider the earlier UK laws mentioned in A above).

The Competition Act 1998 contains two main prohibitions. The Chapter I prohibition prohibits anti-competitive agreements. The Chapter II prohibition prohibits the abuse of a dominant position. These concepts are based on European Union competition law. The Competition Act is enforced by the OFT, which is headed by the Director General of Fair Trading.

2 Anti-competitive agreements: the Chapter I prohibition

2.1 What is prohibited? Chapter I of the Competition Act prohibits agreements between 'undertakings' (meaning any type of business, including sole traders, companies and partnerships) which may affect trade within the UK, and have as their object or effect the prevention, restriction or distortion of competition within the UK, unless they are exempt or excluded.

Any agreement which is prohibited is void and unenforceable. More precisely, the part or parts of it which are prohibited are void. There are complex rules about 'severance' under English law – that is, cutting out parts of agreements, but essentially if what is left can be separated from the prohibited parts without entirely altering the scope and intention of the agreement, the remainder could still stand. But the courts will not rewrite the agreement for the parties.

The Chapter I prohibition is almost identical to Article 81(1) of the Treaty of Rome, to bring UK law into line with EU law. The Competition Act is to be interpreted consistently with EU competition law.

2.2 Key elements In order to use the Chapter I prohibition to get out of an agreement (or important parts of it), you would have to show that the agreement:

- O   affects trade within all or part of the UK;
- O   prevents, restricts or distorts competition;
- O   is not excluded from the Chapter I prohibition;
- O   is not made between parties whose total market share is 25 per cent or less;
- O   is not within a block exemption; and
- O   has not been exempted or cleared by the OFT.

We will consider each of these conditions below.

2.3 What is an 'agreement'? For this purpose, an 'agreement' does not have to be legally binding, nor in writing. But if you are considering whether competition law can help you get out of an agreement, you are probably dealing with a fairly formal agreement.

2.4 The effect on trade For the Chapter I prohibition to apply, the agreement must 'affect trade' within the UK. The effect on trade can be negative or positive, direct or indirect. A potential effect is enough, as long as it would be appreciable. If the agreement affects the structure of the market, it will clearly affect trade.

The 'United Kingdom' includes all or any part of the UK where an agreement operates or is intended to operate. The UK therefore includes every part of England, Wales, Scotland and Northern Ireland. (The Isle of Man and Channel Islands are not included.) Within the UK, no geographic market is too small to be caught: an agreement between two bus companies in Penzance to fix prices or share out routes would be caught if their market shares were high enough.

2.5 Restrictions on competition The Chapter I prohibition applies where the object or effect of the agreement is to prevent, restrict or distort competition. A potential restriction of competition is enough for the Chapter I prohibition to apply, provided the effect is appreciable.

Arguably, any agreement restricts competition because it restricts the parties' freedom to act. But there has to be an appreciable effect on competition before the Chapter I prohibition will apply. This involves considering the economic effect of the agreement, not just its wording. Where the fundamental purpose of the agreement is to eliminate or significantly reduce competition, the prohibition will clearly apply – for example, when two competing builders agree on their responses to an invitation to tender. The agreement is more likely to restrict competition if the parties are actual or potential competitors.

2.6 Examples of anti-competitive agreements The Act gives examples of prohibited agreements. These are agreements:

○   fixing prices or trading conditions;
○   limiting or controlling production, markets, technical development or investment;
○   sharing markets or sources of supply;
○   treating similar customers or suppliers differently, for no good reason; or
○   making a contract conditional on the other party accepting extra unrelated obligations.

These are just examples. One cannot identify every type of agreement which may be prohibited. Each agreement has to be considered within its economic context, from time to time, but three types of agreement are clearly prohibited:

○   price fixing – such as where competing suppliers agree to charge not less than £x per unit for their supplies, or to increase their prices by an agreed percentage;
○   market sharing – for example, where two or more companies agree to allocate customers between them; and

○   resale price maintenance – for example, where a clothing manufacturer tells a retailer not to sell its clothes below a certain price.

2.7 Key exclusions Some types of agreement are excluded from the Chapter I prohibition. In particular, agreements which implement a 'merger' are excluded. (These will include share purchase agreements, business purchase agreements and some joint ventures.) Most agreements which have been registered under the RTPA (see A1 above) are also excluded from the Chapter I prohibition.

The prohibition applies primarily to horizontal agreements. These are agreements between businesses operating at the same stage of the economic process for the purposes of that agreement, such as two bakers. Most vertical agreements (meaning agreements between businesses operating at different economic levels, such as a miller and a baker) do not raise serious competition concerns. All vertical agreements, except those which fix resale prices, have therefore been excluded from the Chapter I prohibition. So have 'land agreements' such as leases, tenancy agreements and licences, along with certain obligations and restrictions relating to land use or transfer.

2.8 Low market shares Where the parties' combined market share is 25 per cent or less, their agreement will generally not have an appreciable effect on competition unless the agreement fixes prices, shares markets between competitors or fixes resale prices. In order to measure market share, one must first define the relevant market. Market definition is considered at B3 below.

2.9 Exemptions and notifications Being 'caught' by the Chapter I prohibition is not necessarily fatal to an agreement – it may be exempt, or capable of being exempted. There are two main types of exemption from the Chapter I prohibition for agreements: block exemptions and individual exemptions. If an agreement is exempt, it is legally enforceable. If the agreement is covered by a block exemption, or has been given individual exemption by the OFT, then the other party or parties to that agreement will almost certainly not be able to use the Competition Act to get out of that agreement.

2.10 Block exemptions A block exemption sets out types of agreement or restrictions which are considered not to be harmful to competition, subject to certain conditions. If an agreement clearly comes within a block exemption, it is exempt from the Chapter I prohibition. There are currently no block exemptions for the UK, but if an agreement is drafted so as to come within a European block exemption, it is automatically exempt from the UK rules. Block exemptions exist under EU law in relation to different types of agreement – for example, vertical agreements (such as purchasing and distribution agreements) and technology transfer agreements.

Block exemptions traditionally set out restrictions on competition which are considered to be acceptable and restrictions which were not permitted. (This is changing, with some categories of agreements being permitted only if the parties' market share is low enough and they do not include prohibited restrictions.)

2.11 Individual exemptions If an agreement is not covered by a block exemption, it may have been granted individual exemption (approval) by the OFT, specifically for that agreement. No approval can be given unless the agreement has been notified to the OFT by one of the parties. An individual exemption will only be given if the agreement has appreciable objective advantages which compensate for any restrictions on competition that it produces. An individual exemption is legally binding for a specified period. An alternative to an individual exemption is a decision from the OFT that the relevant agreement is outside the Chapter I prohibition altogether. Such a decision would prevent the other party to the agreement using the Chapter I prohibition to get out of that agreement. You can check the OFT's website:

www.oft.gov.uk/html/comp-act/case_register/index.html

to see if an agreement has been given individual exemption.

2.12 Transitional provisions Most agreements made before 1 March 2000 are subject to a one-year transitional period from 1 March 2000, during which they will be temporarily excluded from the Chapter I prohibition. No transitional period applies to agreements which were caught by the RTPA if details of those agreements were not provided to the OFT on time; nor is there any transitional period for agreements which are unlawful or void under the RPA. This demonstrates the need to be aware of the pre-1998 law (see A above).

2.13 When does the Chapter I prohibition arise in practice? The Chapter I prohibition is relevant to a wide range of commercial agreements. Cartel arrangements are obviously prohibited. All transactions with competitors need careful consideration, including joint ventures and arrangements to share information. So do trade associations' rules, meetings and conduct. Licences of intellectual property such as trade marks, copyright and patents need to be drafted carefully; and exclusivity provisions and non-compete clauses may also come under attack.

So if, for example, you are a retailer and your agreement with your supplier requires you to charge a particular price for your supplier's products, the Chapter I prohibition will make that requirement unenforceable. It would also negate any agreement between you and an important competitor about who, what or where you would supply, or how you would respond to tenders.

2.14 Key questions In considering whether the Chapter I prohibition could enable you to get out of key parts of your agreement, you therefore need to ask:

O   When was the agreement made?
O   If it was made before 1 March 2000, was it registrable and notifiable under the RTPA? If so, was it properly notified to the OFT?
O   Does it affect trade in the UK?
O   Does it prevent, restrict or distort competition?
O   Is it excluded from the Chapter I prohibition?
O   Does a transitional period apply to it?
O   Has it been given exemption under a block exemption, or individual exemption by the OFT?
O   Is the parties' total market share more than 25 per cent?

3 Abuse of a dominant position: the Chapter II prohibition

3.1 Introduction The Chapter II prohibition could help you get out of an agreement if the other party has considerable market power. The Chapter II prohibition prohibits any conduct by one or more undertakings which amounts to the abuse of a dominant position in a market, if it may affect trade within the UK. It is not dominance which is prohibited, but abuse of that dominance – that is, the misuse of market power.

The Chapter II prohibition is based on Article 82 (previously Article 86) of the Treaty of Rome, which also prohibits the abuse of a dominant position (see Part III, B, below). This is to bring UK law into line with EU law.

There are specific exclusions for certain conduct (including mergers).

3.2 Key elements To use the Chapter II prohibition to get out of an agreement (or important parts of it) you would need to demonstrate that the other party has a dominant position on the relevant market in all or part of the UK; and that making or enforcing the agreement (or relevant parts of it) represents an abuse of that dominant position.

3.3 What is 'dominance'? The European Court of Justice has defined a dominant market position as: 'a position of economic strength ... which enables [an undertaking] to hinder effective competition ... on the relevant market by allowing it to behave ... independently of its competitors, customers and ultimately of consumers'.[5] Power to behave independently in the market is therefore crucial. An alternative test is whether the firm concerned is an 'unavoidable trading partner' so that customers are in effect obliged to deal with it.

To assess whether a firm is dominant, one must first define the relevant product and geographic market. In other words, which type of goods or services are relevant and where? These are defined from the customer's viewpoint, not the producer's. One looks at what customers consider their choices to be. So, if orange juice goes up in price by 10 per cent, will the customers for orange juice buy apple juice, mineral water or Coca-Cola instead?

The product market includes all the products which enough customers consider to be interchangeable, or 'substitutes' for one another – and no others. The geographic market is the area in which similar market conditions apply – that is, choices, prices, suppliers, etc., for the relevant products.

A company accused of abusing a dominant position will try to define the market as widely as possible, to show that it is not dominant – but markets can be defined very narrowly. For example, a company can be dominant in the supply of its own spare parts. Ownership of key intellectual property rights, or an essential facility like an airport, may also give a company a dominant position.

Once the market has been defined, the next consideration is whether the company has enough power on that market to be dominant. Market power is often shown by a high market share compared with competitors. But there is no market share threshold in the Act for defining dominance. Generally, companies with a market share below 40 per cent are unlikely to be regarded as dominant, while a market share of above 50 per cent suggests dominance. Market shares need to be considered over a few years, not just at a particular moment, to assess whether dominance exists. Careful analysis of the relevant market is therefore essential.

Dominance does not come from market share alone. It also depends on other factors, such as the ability to act independently. It is much easier for a dominant company to act independently if it is hard to enter its market (that is, to start competing with it). The level of barriers to entry is therefore important. There may be high costs of entering a new market, which cannot be recovered – licence fees, for example.

3.4 What amounts to abuse? The Act does not prohibit dominant positions. It prohibits the abuse of a dominant position. Abuse generally has two forms: it either exploits dominance, or enhances it by removing or excluding competitors. Abuses generally involve purely unilateral conduct by a dominant organization, while agreements must involve two or more parties; but the Chapter II prohibition can apply to agreements, as an agreement is a form of conduct. The Act gives some examples of what may constitute an abuse. But any conduct by a dominant organization may be abusive if it adversely affects competition, directly or indirectly – even enforcing a contract can be abusive in some circumstances. Examples of abuses which may be featured in agreements include:

O   Charging excessive prices – the obvious way to exploit dominance is to charge excessive prices – that is, prices which bear no reasonable relation to the economic value of the product or service supplied. A dominant company can raise its prices without fear of being undercut. Excessive prices may be featured in agreements – for example, long-term supply contracts. In practice, though, cases involving excessive prices are very rare.

O   Price discrimination – this means charging different prices to different customers for the same product; or charging the same price to customers although the costs of supplying them are different. Either may amount to abuse. An agreement may create price discrimination, either by including different prices within one agreement, or by requiring prices which (when compared with those paid by others) are discriminatory.

O   Fidelity rebates – these can be an abusive method of preventing customers buying from competitors, as they involve rewarding a customer for loyalty. Clauses providing for fidelity rebates could be challenged under the Chapter II prohibition if the supplier has a dominant position.

O   Tie-in sales (or 'bundling') – this is when the purchase of one product is conditional on the purchase of another. This might be included in a purchasing contract: for example if a supplier required a buyer to purchase maintenance services and/or spare parts from the supplier rather than another source, in order to secure products from the supplier.

If these examples cannot be objectively justified, the Director General may find any of them to be an abuse of a dominant position, for which serious fines may be imposed.

When considering whether an agreement (or part of it) is abusive, relevant issues include:

O   What kind of agreement is involved?
O   Does it clearly restrict competition?
O   Is it unfair?
O   Is the relevant agreement normal industry practice?
O   What is its effect on customers and consumers?
O   What is the dominant firm's intention? If it is to respond to a threat, is the agreement proportional to the perceived threat, or does it go too far?

Behaviour – such as including or enforcing particular parts of an agreement – should not be abusive if it has a clear objective justification. For example, discounts which reflect the reduced costs to the supplier of supplying in bulk, rather than a disguised penalty if the buyer buys elsewhere, would not be abusive. But behaviour (or an agreement) which is perfectly acceptable for a company which is not dominant (like price discrimination) may be abusive when done or made by a dominant company.

3.5 When will the Chapter II prohibition arise in practice? The Chapter II prohibition will be relevant to every market in the UK (or any part of it) where one competitor (or a group of competitors) has a high degree of market power. Customers of the dominant player may seek to use the Chapter II prohibition to challenge or defend themselves against abusive conduct: excessive prices, tie-in sales, unfair treatment, and so on.

4 Practical application

So, how could you use the Competition Act to get out of an agreement (or key parts of it)? There are three ways. You could make a complaint to the authorities; bring an action in court; or simply ignore the agreement (or the relevant part of it) and use the Competition Act to defend yourself against the other party's attempts to enforce it.

4.1 Complaints You could complain about the agreement to the relevant authority – usually the Office of Fair Trading. There is no prescribed form for doing so, but the OFT will want to have certain information. A complaint could lead to the parties being forced to modify or terminate the agreement. (It could also lead to the parties being fined up to 10 per cent of their UK turnover for each of the last three years for infringing the Chapter I or Chapter II prohibition.)

The OFT may give a lower priority to complaints about an agreement which are made by one party to that agreement than it gives to complaints by others – for example, competitors. It prioritizes cartel cases – that is, complaints about competitors fixing prices and sharing markets – rather than complaints about agreements which do not involve such blatantly unlawful conduct.

One advantage of complaining about your agreement to the OFT before any other party to it does so is that this could give you immunity from fines. The OFT will give total immunity from fines to the first informant who provides it with evidence of the existence and activities of a cartel, if the OFT has not already started to investigate the infringing agreement or the parties involved. (If the OFT has already started an investigation, it may give total immunity.) But there are conditions: the OFT must not already have enough evidence to prove that the cartel exists; the informant must give all the information and material it has to the OFT, co-operate fully, not have been the leader or instigator and the informant must stop its involvement in the cartel. (Other informants can achieve up to 50 per cent reduction on fines if the

OFT's conditions are satisfied.) If your agreement involved price-fixing or market-sharing, this could be a significant consideration.

Complaints are cheap – but it's up to the OFT whether to listen to them, and when and how to deal with them. Your complaint could therefore be ignored or go nowhere fast.

4.2 Court action You could decide to seize the offensive by bringing a court action in relation to the agreement (or key part[s] of it), seeking a declaration from the court that the agreement is prohibited by the Competition Act 1998 and is therefore unenforceable. Such a declaration would clarify the position. But all court actions are risky. Unlike complaints, court actions are not free. If you lose, you may have to pay your opponent's costs as well as your own. Any goodwill the other party may have had towards you is bound to be lost.

One advantage of litigation is that damages may be recoverable for breaches of the Chapter II prohibition, though no such award has yet been made. But a party to an agreement prohibited by Chapter I of the Competition Act cannot recover damages for loss suffered as a result of that agreement under any circumstances. So, the landlord of a pub owned by a brewer could not recover damages to compensate him for the extra cost of buying beer from the brewer, rather than on the open market, as required by the 'beer tie' provisions in his lease, even if the beer tie was prohibited by Article 81 (the EU equivalent of Chapter I);[6] but this issue has now been referred to the European Court of Justice in another case,[7] so the position may yet change.

For the moment, though, while third parties (such as competitors) can recover damages for breach of the Chapter I prohibition, the parties to the agreement cannot do so, though in theory the non-dominant party could do so for breach of the Chapter II prohibition.

4.3 Ignore the agreement If you have been advised by a specialist lawyer that your agreement (or key part[s] of it) is unenforceable because of the Competition Act, you may prefer simply to ignore the agreement (or those parts) and wait to see what, if anything, the other party does in response. (Whether this is possible will depend on the nature of the agreement or provision in question.) If, for example, the other party then tries to enforce the agreement against you – for example, by suing you – you could then seek to rely on the Competition Act in your defence. One advantage of this approach is that your opponent may decide not to sue you (for example, if it is advised that the agreement is clearly unenforceable or unlawful). You may also delay incurring more legal expenses. But court cases are still risky, even if you are defending them: if you lose, you may have to pay your opponent's costs as well as your own. Also, if the court regards the defence merely as a delaying tactic, it may hear the other party's contractual claim first, leaving your competition-based defence to be tried later.

PART III: EUROPEAN UNION COMPETITION LAW

(A) ARTICLE 81

1 Summary

1.1 What is prohibited? If your agreement affects trade between EU member states,[8] it may be possible to get out of it (or parts of it) using European competition law – especially Article 81 of the Treaty of Rome, which prohibits anti-competitive agreements. Chapter I of the Competition Act 1998 is based on Article 81, so you will find many elements of this section are similar to Part II, B2, dealing with the Chapter I prohibition under the Competition Act 1998.[9]

Article 81(1) prohibits all agreements between undertakings which: 'may affect trade between member states and which have as their object or effect the prevention, restriction or distortion of competition within the Common Market'. Any agreement which is prohibited by Article 81(1) is 'automatically void'. This does not mean the whole of the agreement is necessarily void: just those provisions which are prohibited by Article 81(1). If they can be removed from the rest of the agreement under the national law which applies to that agreement, then what is left of the agreement can remain in force. For example, if an export ban could be deleted from a distributorship agreement, the remaining terms could still stand; but the deleted clause may have been of great commercial importance to the parties.

1.2 Key elements Before you can get out of an agreement (or key parts of it) under Article 81, you need to show that the agreement:

O   affects trade between member states;
O   prevents, restricts or distorts competition;
O   is not 'of minor importance';
O   is not within a block exemption; and
O   has not been exempted or cleared by the Commission.

We will consider each of these five conditions below.

1.3 What is an 'agreement'? An agreement does not have to be in writing to be caught, nor does it have to be legally binding. But if you are considering using Article 81 to get out of an agreement, you are probably dealing with a fairly formal agreement.

2 Effect on trade between member states

The first thing you need to show to get out of an agreement under Article 81 is an effect on trade between member states. This effect may be direct or indirect, actual or potential. This international effect is the extra ingredient which distinguishes EU competition law from the UK's Competition Act 1998.

Any agreement concerning the supply of goods or services from one member state to another (for example, to sell Italian suits in England) obviously affects trade between member states. But there can be an effect on trade between member states even if the parties are all British, because the agreement may make it more difficult for other European businesses to enter into the UK market – especially when other similar agreements are taken into account.

3 Restrictions on competition

The second requirement is that the agreement prevents, restricts or distorts competition, or is intended to do so. A potential restriction of competition is enough for Article 81 to be relevant, provided the effect is appreciable. Some agreements clearly restrict competition: price-fixing and market-sharing cartels are the two most obvious examples. But, in many cases, whether an agreement restricts competition is more arguable. One has to assess the economic effect of the agreement, not just its wording. Where the fundamental purpose of the agreement is to eliminate or significantly reduce competition, then Article 81 will apply – for example, where two competitors agree on their prices. Competition is likely to be restricted where the parties are actual or potential competitors.

Article 81 lists examples of the types of agreements which are prohibited. The list is the same as for the Chapter I prohibition under the Competition Act, and includes price-fixing agreements, agreements controlling resale prices, quota fixing agreements and market-sharing agreements.

One cannot identify every type of agreement which may be prohibited – each agreement has to be considered in its own context, but some agreements or clauses are always prohibited: for example, those which provide for price-fixing; market-sharing; resale price maintenance (attempting to control another party's resale prices); or export bans. Export bans prevent the sale of goods across internal EU borders, or back into the EU. Export bans are prohibited because they divide up the common European market. Creating a single European market is the primary aim of the EU.

4 Agreements of minor importance

Agreements of 'minor importance' are generally not prohibited by Article 81. An agreement is of 'minor importance' if the parties' combined market shares are low enough. There are two thresholds: for 'horizontal' agreements (where the parties are at the same stage in the economic process, such as competing manufacturers) and for agreements which are both horizontal and vertical, or difficult to classify, the threshold is 5 per cent; for 'vertical' agreements (where the parties are at different stages in the economic process), the threshold is 10 per cent. But even if the parties' market shares are low enough, horizontal agreements which are intended to fix prices, limit production or sales, or share markets, and vertical agreements which fix resale prices or give absolute territorial protection, can still be prohibited by Article 81.

5 Block exemptions

Various types of agreements are permitted under a series of 'block exemptions'. If an agreement comes within a block exemption, you will not be able to use Article 81 to get out of it. Originally, block exemptions effectively provided a 'checklist' for the relevant type of agreement – such as exclusive purchasing agreements – by setting out what could and could not be included in it. The recent approach is to permit some categories of agreements if the parties' market share is low enough and they do not include prohibited restrictions.

Block exemptions exist for several major categories of agreements, including 'vertical agreements' (such as purchasing and distribution agreements) specialization agreements; research and development co-operation agreements; and technology transfer agreements (such as patent and know-how licences).

The Commission has also issued several notices which give guidance about the treatment of some types of agreement under Article 81. These include notices concerning some joint ventures; agency agreements; co-operation arrangements; and subcontracting agreements.

6 Individual exemptions/negative clearance

Another thing you need to check, before you can get out of an agreement under Article 81, is whether it has been individually approved by the European Commission. No approval can be given unless the agreement has been notified to the Commission by one of the parties. Your solicitor can find out whether this has been done. The Commission's approval can now be retrospective, that is, with effect from the date of the agreement, not just from the date of the notification. This makes it easier to defend agreements and harder to succeed in challenging them.

Currently only the European Commission can give individual exemptions, although the Commission wants national authorities to be able to do so. The Commission can only exempt an agreement if its benefits outweigh its detrimental effects on competition. An alternative to an exemption is 'negative clearance' – confirmation from the Commission that the relevant agreement is outside the Article 81 prohibition altogether. A decision to that effect would prevent the other party using Article 81 to get out of the agreement. In practice, very few notified agreements get a formal approval decision. Unless an approval decision has been given, the fact that one party has notified an agreement does not stop the other party claiming that key parts of it are unenforceable, either by complaining to the Commission or challenging it in a national court.

Because retrospective exemptions are now possible, if one party challenges an agreement, the other party may respond by notifying it to the Commission.

7 When does Article 81 arise in practice?

Article 81 has been applied to a wide variety of agreements: cartel agreements and export bans are the classic examples, along with agreements which seek to control a reseller's prices. Other examples include: agreements between competitors to share information; joint venture agreements; intellectual property licences; exclusive purchasing agreements, and so on.

In the UK, a large number of cases have involved beer ties – agreements (such as leases of pubs) under which the tenant agrees to buy all its beer from the landlord, or a company specified by the landlord. (In return, the landlord generally gives the tenant a lower rent or some other financial advantage.) Many tenants challenged the tie provisions in their leases, claiming that Article 81 prohibited them. The English courts held that tenants who had made those agreements could not claim damages from the other party, even if those agreements were prohibited by Article 81. Where smaller breweries were involved, the agreements did not affect trade between EU member states and did not have an appreciable effect on competition, even when considered as part of a 'network' of similar agreements.

The practical application of Article 81 is considered further at C below.

(B) ARTICLE 82

1 What is prohibited?

Article 82 of the Treaty of Rome (on which Chapter II of the Competition Act 1998 is based) prohibits abuses of a dominant position. It provides that: 'Any abuse by one or more undertakings of a dominant position within the Common Market or in a substantial part of it shall be prohibited ... in so far as it may affect trade between member states'. Article 82 is therefore intended to prevent the misuse of market power.

2 Key elements

Article 82 involves two elements: first, a 'dominant position'; second, an 'abuse' of that dominant position. Such abuses usually involve purely unilateral conduct, whereas agreements (by definition) involve at least two parties; but Article 82 can apply to agreements.

To use Article 82 to get out of an agreement (or important parts of it) you would need to demonstrate that the other party has a dominant position on the relevant market in all or a substantial part of the EU; that making or enforcing the agreement (or relevant parts of it) represented an abuse of that dominant position; and the abuse has had, or is capable of having, a significant effect on trade between EU member states.

3 What is 'dominance'?

A dominant market position has been defined by the European Court of Justice as: 'a position of economic strength ... which enables [an undertaking] to hinder ... effective competition ... on the relevant market by allowing it to behave ... independently of its competitors, customers and ultimately of consumers'. So power to behave independently in the market is crucial. An alternative test is whether the firm concerned is an 'unavoidable trading partner' so that customers have no option but to deal with it.

To assess whether a firm is dominant, one must first define the relevant product and geographic market. This process is the same as under the Chapter II prohibition – see Part II, B3, above. Essentially, the customer's viewpoint is what matters. Markets have sometimes been defined very narrowly for this purpose. For example, a company can be dominant in the market for the supply of its own spare parts. Ownership of key intellectual property rights (for example, the copyright in the television programme schedules) or essential facilities (such as a port) may also confer dominance.

Once the market has been defined, the next issue is whether the company has enough power to be dominant in that market. Market power is often shown by a high market share compared with competitors. But Article 82 does not specify the market share level at which dominance exists. The European Commission treats companies with a market share of 50 per cent or more as probably dominant and those with less than 40 per cent as unlikely to be dominant. Market shares need to be considered over a few years, not just at a particular moment, to assess whether dominance exists. Careful analysis of the relevant market is therefore essential.

Whether a company is dominant on a particular market depends upon whether it can behave independently of its competitors and customers in that market. It is much easier for a dominant company to act independently if it is hard to enter its market (that is, to start competing with it). This makes the level of barriers to entry important – for example, how expensive is it to enter the market? What does one need to do so?

The 'special ingredient' for Article 82 to apply (as opposed to UK competition law) is the European element. The dominant position must apply in the whole of the EU, or in a 'substantial part' of it. Generally, one of the larger member states (such as the UK) will be a 'substantial part' of the EU, but what is 'substantial' depends on the product or service concerned: the City of London would be a substantial part of the EU for certain financial products or services, but not for breakfast cereals!

4 Abuse

It is not illegal to have a dominant position. Article 82 prohibits the abuse of that dominant position. Abuse generally either exploits dominance, or enhances it by removing or excluding competitors. Abuses generally involve purely unilateral conduct by a dominant organization, while agreements must involve two or more parties; but Article 82 can apply to agreements.

What constitutes an abuse? Article 82 itself gives some examples of abusive conduct. The list is the same as for the Chapter II prohibition (see Part II, B3.4, above). It includes imposing unfair purchase or selling prices or other unfair trading conditions and limiting production, markets or technical development to the prejudice of consumers.

Any conduct by a dominant organization may be abusive if it adversely affects competition, directly or indirectly – even enforcing a contract can be abusive in some circumstances.

Examples of abuse were considered earlier in relation to the Chapter II prohibition (see Part II, B3.4, above). They include charging excessive prices, price discrimination, fidelity rebates and tie-in sales.

When considering whether an agreement (or part of it) is abusive, relevant issues include:

○   What kind of agreement is involved?
○   Does it clearly restrict competition? Is it unfair?
○   Is it normal industry practice?
○   What is its effect on customers and consumers?
○   What is the dominant firm's intention? If it is to respond to a threat, is the agreement proportional to the perceived threat, or does it go too far?
○   Does the agreement go against the general principles of the EU – for example, the desire to eliminate national boundaries and to avoid discrimination between people from different member states?

The *Tetra Pak* case[10] provides several examples of abuses of a dominant position. Tetra Pak had a very high market share for packaging liquids (such as fruit juice) in cardboard cartons. It required customers of its liquid-food processing machines to use only Tetra Pak's cartons in those machines. It forbade its customers to modify or move the packaging equipment, or to use it in conjunction with other machinery, even where the equipment had been purchased outright. Tetra Pak also claimed the exclusive right to supply spare parts both for purchased and rented machines. Monthly maintenance fees were adjusted to reflect the client's loyalty to Tetra Pak, rather than the amount of servicing actually required. Tetra Pak also imposed minimum rental periods of between three and nine years, which were held to be unacceptable. Each of these practices was held to be an abuse of its dominant position and therefore unlawful.

Behaviour – such as including or enforcing particular parts of an agreement – should not be abusive if it has a clear objective justification. For example, discounts which reflect the reduced costs to the supplier of supplying in bulk, rather than a disguised penalty if the buyer buys elsewhere, would not be abusive. But behaviour (or an agreement) which is perfectly acceptable for a company which is not dominant (like price discrimination) may be abusive when done or made by a dominant company.

5 The effect on trade

You have to show an effect on trade between member states before you can rely on Article 82. This effect can be direct or indirect, actual or potential. But the UK courts have been more reluctant to find an effect on inter-state trade than the European authorities, particularly if both parties are British.

If you cannot show an obvious effect on inter-state trade, it would generally be advisable to seek to rely on the Competition Act, as the Chapter II prohibition is essentially the same as Article 82, without the requirement to show an effect on trade between member states.

6 No exemptions

It is not possible to obtain an exemption from the European Commission for the abuse of a dominant position. But as 'abuse' is a flexible concept, the authorities may, if they wish, excuse conduct by not classifying it as an abuse. However, it is possible for a negative clearance decision to be issued by the Commission, where the Commission certifies that on the basis of the facts known to it there are no grounds for proceeding under Article 82.

7 When does Article 82 arise in practice?

Article 82 is relevant to every market in the EU (or substantial parts of it, such as the UK) where one competitor (or a group of competitors) has a high degree of market power. But for the Chapter II prohibition, the abuse of market power must have at least a potential effect on trade between EU member states. The geographic market involved needs to be fairly large – much larger than for the Chapter II prohibition to apply. Competitors or customers of the dominant player may seek to use Article 82 to challenge or defend themselves against abusive conduct: excessive prices, tie-in sales, unfair treatment and so on.

(C) PRACTICAL APPLICATION OF ARTICLES 81 AND 82

So, how could you use Articles 81 and 82 to get out of an agreement (or key parts of it)? There are three ways: you could make a complaint to the authorities; bring an action in court; or simply ignore the agreement (or the relevant part of it) and use Articles 81 and 82 to defend yourself against the other party's attempts to enforce it.

1 Complaints

You could complain about the agreement to the relevant authority – generally the European Commission. There is an optional form for complaints to the

Commission (the form [Form C] can be obtained from the Commission's Information Offices, which are at Jean Monet House, 8 Storey's Gate, London SW1P 3AT). A complaint could lead to the parties being forced to modify or terminate the agreement. It could also lead to the parties being fined up to 10 per cent of their turnover for infringing Article 81 or 82.

The European Commission may give a lower priority to complaints about an agreement which are made by one party to that agreement than it gives to complaints by others – for example, competitors. The European Commission generally prioritizes cartel cases – that is, complaints about competitors fixing prices and sharing markets – rather than complaints about agreements which do not involve such blatantly unlawful conduct.

One advantage of complaining about your agreement to the European Commission before any other party to it does so is that this could give you immunity from fines. The European Commission will give the first informant about a secret cartel immunity from fines if it was not already investigating the infringing agreement and (among other things) the informant was not the ringleader. If your agreement involved secret price-fixing or market-sharing, this could be a significant consideration.

Complaints are cheap – but it's up to the European Commission whether to listen to them, and when and how to deal with them. Your complaint could therefore be ignored or go nowhere fast.

2 Court action

You could decide to seize the offensive by bringing a court action in a national court in relation to the agreement (or key part[s] of it), seeking a declaration from the court that the agreement is prohibited by the Articles 81 and/or 82 and is therefore unenforceable. Such a declaration would clarify the position. But all court actions are risky. Unlike complaints, court actions are not free. If you lose, you may have to pay your opponent's costs as well as your own. Any goodwill the other party may have had towards you is bound to be lost.

One advantage of litigation is that damages may be recoverable for breaches of Article 82, though no such award has yet been made in the English courts. But a party to an agreement prohibited by Article 81 cannot recover damages for loss suffered as a result of that agreement under any circumstances. So, the landlord of a pub owned by a brewer could not recover damages to compensate him for the extra cost of buying beer from the brewer, rather than on the open market, as required by the 'beer tie' provisions in his lease, even if the beer tie was prohibited by Article 81;[11] but this issue has now been referred to the European Court of Justice in another case,[12] so the position may yet change.

For the moment, though, while third parties (such as competitors) can recover damages for breach of Article 81, the parties to the agreement cannot do so, though in theory the non-dominant party could do so for breach of Article 82.

3 Ignore the agreement

If you have been advised by a specialist lawyer that your agreement (or key part[s] of it) is unenforceable because of Articles 81 and/or 82, you may prefer simply to ignore the agreement (or those parts) and wait to see what, if anything, the other party does in response. (Whether this is possible will depend on the nature of the agreement or provision in question.) If, for example, the other party then tries to enforce the agreement against you – for example, by suing you – you could then seek to rely on Articles 81 and/or 82 in your defence.

The main advantages of this approach are that your opponent may not sue you (for example, if it is advised that the agreement is clearly unenforceable or unlawful) and that you may delay your legal expenses. But court cases are still risky, even if you are defending them: if you lose, you may have to pay your opponent's costs as well as your own. Also, if the court regards the defence merely as a delaying tactic, it may hear the other party's contractual claim first, leaving your competition-based defence to be tried later.

To date, English courts have generally been hostile to attempts by one party to an agreement to use a 'Euro-defence' to escape its contractual obligations: they have, for example, been more reluctant than the European Commission or the European courts to find an effect on trade between member states. But this does not mean that a defence (or claim) based on Articles 81 and/or 82 will inevitably fail; indeed, as English courts become more used to competition issues because of the Competition Act 1998, they may become more receptive to arguments based on EU competition law.

PART IV: CONCLUSIONS

1   So what does all this highly technical law mean? If you're trying to get out of an agreement, do not overlook competition law. If the other party has ignored it, you could use this to your advantage. This means that when you are making an agreement and you want the other side to be bound by it, make sure you take advice on any competition law implications before the deal is signed.

2   If the agreement was made before 1 March 2000, was registrable under the RTPA and details were not given to the OFT on time, relevant restrictions in it will be unenforceable.

3   If the agreement – or key parts of it – are prohibited by the Competition Act, or Article 81 or 82, then those parts will be unenforceable. This could allow you to walk away from your contractual obligations.

These may not be the nicest tactics in the world, but those are the rules: and sometimes they can be very useful.

4   In practice, there are three ways of using competition law to get out of an agreement: the first is to complain about the agreement to the competition authorities – the OFT or European Commission. If they pursue the complaint, they may decide that the agreement (or key parts of it) are unenforceable. But they may not pursue your complaint, or may take too long to do so. They will generally be more interested in complaints from third parties (such as competitors) than from the parties to an agreement. The second method is to bring court proceedings for a declaration that the agreement (or key parts of it) are legally prohibited – by the Competition Act or by Articles 81 and/or 82. Like all litigation, this strategy has risks (see Chapter 8). The third option is to treat the agreement (or key parts of it) as being void and ignore it – if the other party then sues you for breach, rely on competition law as a defence.

5   If all the parties to the agreement are British and the effects of the agreement are felt entirely in the UK, then try to rely on the Competition Act, rather than Articles 81 and/or 82. But if the other party is from elsewhere in Europe and the agreement's effects occur elsewhere in the EU, as well as (or instead of) the UK, then EU law may be more appropriate. There is a considerable degree of overlap, but there is no need to show an effect on trade between member states if you rely on the Competition Act. In practice, therefore, it may well be easier to rely on the Competition Act, especially when doing business in the UK.

NOTES

1   Austria, Belgium, Denmark, Finland, France, Germany, Greece, Ireland, Italy, Luxembourg, the Netherlands, Portugal, Spain, Sweden and the UK.

2   These were renumbered by the Treaty of Amsterdam; they were originally Articles 85 and 86.

3   *MD Foods* (formerly Associated Dairies Ltd) v. *Baines* [1997] 1 All ER 833.

4   *Topliss Showers Ltd* v. *Gessey & Son Ltd* [1982] ICR 501.

5   Case 27/76 *United Brands* v. *EC Commission* [1978] ECR 207.

6   *Gibbs Mew* v. *Gemmell*, CA, 22 July 1998 [1998] Eu LR 588, [1999] ECC 97.

7   *Inntrepreneur and Courage* v. *Crehan*, CA, 27 May 1999, [1999] EGCS 85, (1999) 96 (25) LSG 29.

8   Austria, Belgium, Denmark, Finland, France, Germany, Greece, Ireland, Italy, Luxembourg, the Netherlands, Portugal, Spain, Sweden and the UK.

9   Under Chapters 52 and 53 of the European Economic Area (EEA) Agreement, identical rules to Articles 81 and 82 of the Treaty of Rome apply in the EEA. The EEA comprises the 15 member states of the EU, plus Iceland, Liechtenstein and Norway. Rather than refer to the EEA and the EEA Agreement throughout, we will refer to the EU and Articles 81 and 82.

10   Case C-333/94P *Tetra Pak International SA* v. *EC Commission* [1997] All ER (EC) 4.

11   *Gibbs Mew* v. *Gemmell*, CA, 22 July 1998, [1998] Eu LR 588.

12   *Inntrepreneur and Courage* v. *Crehan*, CA, 27 May 1999, [1999] EGCS 85.

6

TERMINATION FOR BREACH

THE BASIC RULES

If nothing is expressly agreed in a contract, the legal rules provide a complex matrix against which each set of facts must be tested. The basic legal rule is that a breach of 'condition' by one party (or, to put it in different words, a serious breach) allows the other to terminate. The effect of terminating the contract because of the other side's breach is that the 'innocent party' is let off (or, to use the legal term, 'discharged') from further performing its side of the deal – whilst preserving the right to sue for damages caused by the breach of contract before termination (and, as is shown in Chapter 8, often for damages that result from the fact that once the contract is ended, the other side is no longer performing what it was contracted to do).

The breach of contract rarely, by itself, brings the contract to an end – it is usually up to the other party (the non-breaching or innocent party) to decide whether to rely on the breach as a reason for terminating – but it will usually also be a free choice for the non-breaching or innocent party to elect to continue with the contract despite the breach.

If the innocent party does choose to bring the contract to an end, it must communicate that decision to the other party – and the points which were covered in Chapter 4 about giving notices (to whom, in particular, but not the period of notice, of course) will apply equally here.

The most difficult part of the process for the innocent party is that it must make sure that it does nothing inconsistent with its decision to terminate the contract – if it does otherwise, a court might well find that the contract continued, or even that a new contract had been created. Continuing to deliver goods or perform services when the other party is in breach might lead to the fact that its claim that the contract is over is itself ignored by the courts.

A detailed analysis of the case law on what is (and what is not) a 'condition' (as distinguished from a 'warranty', which if broken entitles the other party to damages only) or what is a serious breach is beyond the scope of this book, but for these purposes what follows should help give a feel for the general framework in which lawyers and the courts are working.

Nowadays, contract terms are classified as being conditions, warranties or (in as unhelpful a way as possible), 'innominate or intermediate' terms – in other words, neither conditions nor warranties, but something somewhere in between and being treated as a condition or a warranty as the circumstances require! If one of these other, intermediate terms is broken, the courts will decide whether the term is of a condition-type, being so serious that it deprives the party not in breach of so much of the purpose of having entered the contract and entitles the 'innocent' or 'injured' party the right to terminate the contract and claim damages, or whether the term is of a warranty-type, and so only allows the innocent or injured party the right to claim damages.

Obviously, if you are about to take a decision based on whether the other party's breach is of a type of clause which allows you to terminate, knowing whether the clause is of that type or not would help! The consequence for you of getting it wrong and treating the contract as ended when, in fact, the other party's breach was of a less serious term could result in the other party being able to sue you for having walked away from the contract with no good (that is, legal) reason! In commercial affairs, the effect of the breach of a term may be less serious than the same breach in the circumstances where the buyer is not another commercial organization but where he or she is a consumer.

Because of the possible uncertainty of knowing if a particular term is a condition or not, the key message is that if the parties can agree at the contract stage what obligations are conditions, the more likely it will be that termination for breach of any of those obligations will stand up if challenged in court. If a particular type of term is standard in a given industry then it is likely to have been given an agreed (that is, industry-accepted) classification – namely as a condition, a warranty or an intermediate term – and unless the parties make it plain that they are using that type of clause in some other sense, it will be treated in the industry-accepted way.

In deciding whether a term is to be treated as a condition or warranty (or other type of term), the relevant time at which (in an ideal world) a court would want to ask the parties what their intention is, is at the time that the parties are making their contract, and not (with the advantage of hindsight) when the breach happens and the consequences of that breach are known. Obviously, at the time of the making of the contract, the parties will have, if only at the backs of their minds, thoughts as to what might happen if the other party were to break its promise somewhere along the line, and those nagging thoughts are likely to dictate, at least in some part, whether the particular promise is to be a condition or a warranty. Having stated that theoretical basis for determining the status for a promise, it will only be relevant, in the contractual sense, if the party which is thinking that the other's promise is very important actually says as much before the contract is made.

The truth, unfortunately, is that there is an increasing trend to treat all terms as innominate or intermediate, and we will come to what that means shortly; although this book is not meant to be an academic legal textbook on the whys and wherefores of modern English law, the reader should at least note that there are reasons for the modern trend towards the neutral classification (even if this trend makes the lawyer's job potentially less straightforward, and the client's wallet slightly lighter!). The advantage of allowing the parties to agree on classification gives the contract a certainty at the outset; however it also means that even a trivial breach of a promise, which was classified at the time of making the contract as a condition but which turns out not to be that important a few weeks later, can allow the 'innocent' party to terminate and get out of the agreement, which does not make for particularly stable relationships and (but let us not be too cynical!) gives the judges less interesting work to do! In one case in the mid-1970s,[1] the Court of Appeal based its objection to treating terms as conditions too readily as 'in principle, contracts are made to be performed and not to be avoided according to the whims of market fluctuations', and went on to state that, given a choice between treating a term as a condition or an intermediate term, 'the court should tend to prefer the construction which will ensure performance and not encourage avoidance of contractual obligations'. It is interesting to note that five years later, the House of Lords (the highest English court), made clear[2] that 'in suitable cases, if the intention of the parties so indicates' a promise should have 'the force of a condition'.

So, to summarize the position reached so far in this chapter – promises which make it into the contract might be conditions, warranties or innominate terms. The parties might agree on classification, or there might be industry-standard treatments but, otherwise, it is up to the courts to decide the issue. Because the classification of terms is so important to your ability to get out of a contract, we will look in a bit more depth at some of the issues that the courts have considered over the years, although you could skip over the next few paragraphs and rejoin where the three examples are set out. (Once you have read those examples, you might decide to skip back to here!).

We have noted that the parties may call one (or more) of the provisions of their contract a 'condition', but (perhaps unsurprisingly) the courts have sometimes decided that even where the parties have expressly designated some particular term to be a condition, there is a difference between what a lawyer means by a word and what a (to denigrate our profession!) human being means. This Humpty Dumpty world-view of things does have some merit: what the courts are trying to get to the bottom of is what the parties intended by their words, and sometimes, despite their best efforts, the parties will use a word (such as 'condition') which has a very precise meaning in some other sense. Remember, if a term really is a condition, its breach (however trivial, in fact or in consequence) allows the other party to terminate the agreement, so it is important that the courts keep the system going by not readily allowing very unreasonable results to flow.

We have also noted that, increasingly, terms are being treated as intermediate terms, because that classification gives the court flexibility as to the result of breach of that term, depending on the consequences of breach rather than the labelling of the term. The questions that the courts ask are various, but include whether breach of the term goes to the root of the contract (or, in other words, would A have entered the contract if B had not made whatever that particular promise is), and whether the breach was serious and substantial – with expert opinion being called in to help determine whether the deviation in what actually happened from what was contracted to happen is such as to allow the innocent, injured party its ultimate contractual right: to get out of the agreement. In many contracts, the parties are given specific rights to terminate their agreement, and those specific rights might be in addition to, or in place of, the right to terminate for breach by the other party of a condition of the contract.

Further analysis can be found in any substantial contract law textbook, but here are some examples from the decided cases, and which give some of the flavour of the issues the courts would be looking at.

EXAMPLE 1

In an 1841 case,[3] the court's argument was that the more important the term was to the contract, the more likely it would be that it would be classified as a condition of the contract.

EXAMPLE 2

In an 1863 case,[4] it was important to the ship's hirer that the ship was 'in the port of Amsterdam'. In fact, it was not there; and the court found that term to be a condition.

EXAMPLE 3

In a more recent case[5] (decided in 1981), the seriousness of the consequence flowing from the breach of the term was the thing that decided whether the particular term was a condition or not.

BREACH OF OBLIGATION

Although lawyers are often thought of as picking arguments simply for the sake of it, some parts of contracts will always draw particular attention from the legal advisers. One of the areas in negotiating a contract that often takes up considerable time (and legal fees) turns on the following four possible phrases:

1   'breach of any obligation by the Supplier entitles the Customer to terminate'. The Supplier is likely to resist this language: any breach of any obligation, however insubstantial, will allow the Customer to terminate the contract. This probably goes further than even the Customer really wants, but it is likely to be the Customer's starting point in negotiations.

    The example used to illustrate (1) and (3) is this: it is common to include within the notices clause (which we have looked at in Chapter 2) a provision that if the party's address for service of notices changes, that party must notify the other party of the change of details. Nothing really (in fact, to be frank, nothing at all) turns on whether a change of address card is sent. Yet a failure to send it would amount to a 'breach of any obligation'. If the Supplier moved and failed to notify the Customer, a straightforward reading of the clause would entitle the Customer to terminate the contract. Obviously that was never what either party would have intended, but getting both parties (and sometimes even their legal advisers) to agree the common sense of this proposition can sometimes take considerable time.

2   'breach of any material obligation by the Supplier entitles the Customer to terminate'. Note the introduction of the word 'material' – it adds a description to the type of obligation which actually matters. This is often a compromise solution. It protects the Supplier from the risk of termination for its failure to do something immaterial. It also recognizes that the Customer has a real interest in that obligation being performed. What is (and what is not) a 'material' obligation can be left open or spelled out in the contract. There are good arguments for adopting either position; agreeing which obligations are material focuses the parties' minds on what is important, but (unless very carefully drawn up) a failure to include an obligation in the agreed list of 'material' things will condemn that event to being treated as not immaterial and so it will not be a trigger event allowing the other party to terminate the agreement. One thing must be added by way of a counterbalance to that view however: what seems immaterial at the negotiation stage might be

most material one year down the line. Conversely, leaving the matter open simply returns the parties to the basic legal rule – because, as we have already seen in this chapter, a 'material obligation' is a 'condition'.

3   'material breach of any obligation by the Supplier entitles the Customer to terminate'. The example in (1) is useful here. The failure to notify a change of address is a material (that is, a total) breach of the obligation to notify a change of address. And, as has been seen in example (1), that is in neither party's real interests. This suggested wording for the clause, therefore, does not really take things forward.

4   'material breach of any material obligation by the Supplier entitles the Customer to terminate'. This phraseology protects the Supplier most out of the four options. It means that both the extent of the breach (it has to be a 'material breach') and the importance of the obligation are taken into account (it has to be a 'material obligation'). Again, defining exactly what constitutes a 'material breach' and what are the 'material obligations' adds certainty, but might prevent termination if insufficiently widely drawn up, and so defeats the very purpose that the Customer wanted to achieve!

One key issue that must be noted in relation to any contractual right to terminate is that when notice of the termination is required to be given to terminate the contract, the notice, as well as being properly given, must state what the breach is and, if there is a right to remedy (see below), that the failure to remedy the breach in the correct time frame (which is something that ought to be stated in the contract) will result in termination.

Before turning to further issues surrounding breach – namely, 'persistent breach' and considering any right to remedy breaches – it is worth pausing to make a distinction between what we have been considering (namely breach of obligations) and non-performance of the contract. That distinction is well illustrated by a case from 1838,[6] where the judge stated:

> If a man offers to buy the peas off another, and he sends him beans, he does not perform his contract. But that is not a warranty; there is no warranty that he should sell him peas; the contract is to sell peas, and if he sends him anything else in their stead, it is a non-performance of it.

In other words, the non-performance by the seller means that the buyer can treat himself as let off (or, to use the legal terminology, discharged from) the contract. There is, in this example, no breach of warranty or condition or intermediate term, simply a straightforward non-performance.

THE BAKERY SCENARIO

There are two facts in the Bakery Scenario that merit attention here: first, the late delivery of ovens 4 and 5 (which were due to be delivered on 10

December but only arrived on 20 December, giving no time to get those bakeries up and running before the New Year period), and second, that the ovens were unreliable, in that although they were capable of producing edible bread and cake, this was only because rough and ready manual settings could (and had to) be used and, in addition, one of the ovens was proving hard and slow to clean.

Would late delivery entitle Supermarket to reject the ovens? There is a concept in English law called 'time of the essence', which, if it applies to the contract, means that the late doing of something does entitle the other party to reject or terminate.

In a commercial context, where time is not expressly stated to be 'of the essence', one party can nonetheless have made clear to the other that time was a key issue. In the Bakery Scenario, there seems little doubt that Supermarket did make it very clear that it needed delivery of working ovens in good time for the launch date. As Supermarket did not reject the late deliveries of ovens, it lost its chance to treat the contract as ended, and instead needs to rely on the remedies afforded to an 'injured' contracting party, as explained in Chapter 8. In relation to the shoddy goods, Supermarket does have an opportunity in law to test them, and given that the ovens do not work, that could (if it is not now too late) give Supermarket the right to treat that as a material breach of the contract, entitling it to terminate the contract and seek damages.

PERSISTENT BREACHES

Another situation that the Customer might want to cover is the persistent breach by the Supplier. In the Garage Scenario, George might (with hindsight) have wanted to cover the persistent delays in Max making payment: in other words, he would like to have the right to terminate as a result of the regular failure to make payment. Here, no one breach is enough to justify termination, but a given number of repeated breaches over a stated period of time might suffice. A clear definition (for example, 'four breaches in any six-month period') of how this yellow card/red card regime is to work is advisable. The 'persistent breach' approach can, however, introduce its own debating points: is it any breach, however minor, which counts, or must the breach be of a certain type or seriousness? If the type of breach has to be of a given importance to count, one could go through the 'material breach'/ 'material obligation' debate all over again. What also often happens in negotiations leading to the contract being finalized is that the parties agree the principal of dealing with persistent breach, but then find themselves spending considerable amounts of time and money arguing over whether a breach that occurs in one month is, for example, wiped clean by a good performance in the next (or various versions of that debate).

RIGHT TO REMEDY

It is usual to include in a clause which entitles one party to terminate if the other fails to perform an obligation a right for the party in breach to fix the breach. Of course, only breaches capable of remedy can benefit from such a right.

Assuming that it is the Supplier that is in breach, the Customer might be willing to give it 14 days, or some longer or shorter period, to fix the breach. Some obligations will be so critical that no fix time is acceptable, or only a very short period. Other obligations will not even lend themselves to fix times. For example, in a computer contract, the system might be the subject of a support agreement, which requires the Supplier to respond to fault calls within, say, three hours, and (if the Customer is very lucky) to fix the fault within six hours. Whereas a failure to respond to a call in three hours and 15 minutes might not be critical, and might be remedied by some form of monthly fee reduction, the failure to fix within six hours and a minute might be catastrophic for the Customer, and remedying the breach (namely, fixing it within a further two hours beyond the six hours) so wholly unacceptable that the Customer would not enter into an agreement where that was the only remedy that the Supplier was prepared to agree.

The Supplier might seek to extend the fix time: for example, if it has started to fix the breach and continues to use all reasonable endeavours to fix the breach, it will argue that the Customer cannot terminate. That might be in many cases unacceptable to the Customer. If agreed to, the Customer is not getting some aspect of the service for which it is paying a fee and yet cannot terminate. A Customer should seek to avoid this type of clause: it gives the Supplier considerable leeway without a final sanction reserved for the Customer.

MOTIVE NOT RELEVANT

Just because the Supplier (say) intentionally breaks its contractual obligation, the Customer does not necessarily have the right to walk away from the contract. In one case, the hirer of a ship had intentionally, and in breach of its contractual obligation, delayed loading the ship for a day. The ship's owner could not terminate the contract, and the court held that, instead, the owner was perfectly well protected by an award of damages. The question of the guilty party's intentions or frame of mind is not relevant to the issue of entitlement to terminate or to damages.

In a number of property cases, the seller has intentionally (and, in fact, fraudulently) overstated the plot's size. In those cases, the buyer could treat the contract as so broken that the buyer could terminate it and, here, the courts have not tried to force the buyer to keep the small plot, plus damages. (Had the overstatement been made innocently, the courts would have followed that route – and that is why when buying a property, having it properly surveyed is an important part of the process.)

Lawyers refer to the situation in which one party makes it clear that it no longer wishes to be bound by the contract as 'repudiation'. Repudiation is a form of intentional breach: the Customer (for example), in one case, told the Supplier that, although he had contracted to pay cash on delivery, he would start paying after delivery in future, and the Supplier did not need to put up with that. (Of course the flip side is equally true: if the Supplier had announced that it would only deliver goods in future if, having contracted on terms requiring cash on delivery, it sought payment before it delivered future consignments.) But care must be taken when relying on the other party's apparent repudiation: in a number of cases, one party (A) has taken a course of action, in good faith, which the other (B), wrongly, took as a repudiation – the effect of that was that party B's action in declaring the contract at an end was itself a repudiation, entitling party A to end the contract. It is hard to imagine a more unfortunate situation in which Party B could have found itself: A had done something B was not wanting, and as a result of its own consequent and precipitous action, B found itself in breach of the contract.

The thing to be aware of in this brief discussion is that it is not only a repudiation to refuse to be bound by the contract's term, it can also be a repudiation to agree to meet the contract, but only in a manner which is at odds with the obligations in the contract.

Sometimes, part of a contract has been performed, but that does not prevent one party from terminating. In *Sumpter* v. *Hedges*,[7] the builder stopped work part way through a building project on the defendant's land. As the defendant had no option but to accept the building as it then stood, the builder failed in its claim for payment for what it had actually built when the landowner terminated the contract.

INSOLVENCY

It is usual to provide that either party may terminate the contract if the other is insolvent. That need not be the same as being in a formal insolvency regime (such as liquidation, receivership, administration, bankruptcy), but simply unable to pay its debts as they fall due.

A full discussion and definition of the language of insolvency may be found in the specialist textbooks. But as the terminology of insolvency is often used, we thought we should at least mention the key terms, and also briefly clarify their meanings.

'Bankruptcy' is a term that is applicable only to individuals. It will have no application to most commercial agreements, but if one party is a sole trader, then it will be relevant. An individual who is a major shareholder of either party could be a party to the contract: his or her bankruptcy could be sufficiently important to the other side to justify it terminating the contract, but only if he or she is a party to the contract or if his or her insolvency is included within the contract as giving the other party such a right. It is not uncommon in contracts with small companies, or ones with limited trading histories, to seek and obtain a guarantee from the main shareholder. The bankruptcy of that main shareholder should be something, the happening of which, the other party would want to be able to use, to terminate the contract – but unless that is a contract term, there will be no automatic right to terminate on that ground.

United States-drafted contracts might include reference to 'Chapter 11' or 'Chapter 7'. These are chapters (or sections) of the applicable US law, and roughly equate to the English insolvency procedures of administrative receivership and administration.

NOTES

1   Hansa Nord [1976] QB 44.
2   *Bunge* v. *Tradax* [1981] 1 WLR 711.
3   *Glaholm* v. *Hays* (1841) 10 LJCP 98.
4   *Behn* v. *Burness* (1863) 32 LJQB 204.
5   *Bunge* v. *Tradax* [1981] 1 WLR 711.
6   *Chanter* v. *Hopkins* [1838] 4 M&W 399.
7   *Sumpter* v. *Hedges* [1898] 1 QB 673.

7

MISREPRESENTATION AND WAIVER

INTRODUCTION TO MISREPRESENTATION

What if one party has been induced to enter into a contract by a statement made or information provided by another and that statement or information turns out to have been misleading and/or inaccurate? What remedies, if any, are available to the innocent party? In particular, is the innocent party entitled to pull out of the contract?

The short answer is that if the statement made was sufficiently important to induce and did induce the innocent party to enter into the contract and the statement is false then the law allows the innocent party an opportunity to pull out of the contract. The law recognizes that there has been a fundamental defect in the formation (not performance) of the contract.

In Chapters 4 and 6 we looked at how a statement made during negotiations could be interpreted as being a term of the contract. Alternatively the statement may form the basis of a separate collateral contract between the parties.

If the statement is a contractual term or a collateral contract has been formed, the remedy for non-compliance (that is, in this context, a false promise) is breach of contract. Breach of contract by one party will entitle the innocent party to an award of damages and possibly the right to terminate the contract (depending upon whether the term that has been breached is a condition, a warranty or an intermediate term).

If the statement falls short of being a contract term, and no collateral contract has been formed, it is classified as representation. We are concerned in this chapter with false representations (that is, 'misrepresentations') – being statements that have not become contract terms.

If you are the victim of inaccurate or misleading pre-contract representations, you need to consider what remedies may be available to you within the law of misrepresentation. Unfortunately the law in this area (partly statute and partly case law) might seem to be unnecessarily complex. In this chapter we will endeavour to simply highlight some of the key issues to consider when exploring whether misrepresentation may provide you with an exit route to get out of a contract.

Take the example of our unfortunate car dealer George. In commercial terms, he struck a deal with Max in the hope/expectation that as Max's business expanded, Max would buy new cars for his fleet from George. Max made it clear from the outset that this was his intention. The rental business and the fleet did expand but the new cars for the fleet were not purchased from George. Can George look to cancel his maintenance contract on the basis that he was duped by Max?

WHAT CONSTITUTES AN ACTIONABLE MISREPRESENTATION?

There are an infinite variety of inaccurate or misleading pre-contract statements that could, in a non-legal sense, be termed 'misrepresentations'. However, the law of misrepresentation will only provide a remedy to the innocent party if the statement in question falls within strict parameters. It must be a false statement of some specific existing fact or past event. Any other type of statement cannot be an actionable misrepresentation for legal purposes. So for example none of the following types of statements can constitute an actionable misrepresentation:

O   a statement of opinion;
O   a statement of future conduct or intention;
O   a statement of law; or
O   mere sales talk.

STATEMENT OF FACT OR OPINION?

On occasions it can be difficult to ascertain whether a statement is a positive assertion that a particular fact is true or a statement of the maker's opinion or belief.

Take an example from the leading case in this area of the law.[1] A seller of land notified a potential buyer that the land had a capacity to support 2000 sheep. Was this a statement of fact or an expression of the maker's opinion? On the facts of this case, the court decided that the statement was an opinion only. Although the seller was a farmer, he was not a sheep farmer. The innocent party knew that the maker of the statement had no special knowledge of sheep farming and was doing no more than expressing an opinion.

A statement may appear to be one of opinion but if it is not honestly held it will be treated as a statement of fact. For example, what if the seller of a painting insists that he thinks that a particular painting is an original Rembrandt when in fact he knows it to be a copy? Is this a statement of opinion or fact? It is a statement of fact. It is a misrepresentation of fact for a person to say that he holds an opinion that he does not hold.[2]

STATEMENT OF FUTURE CONDUCT OR INTENTION

The basic rule is that a representation as to a party's intention or future conduct cannot give rise to a cause of action for misrepresentation. (It may, of course, form the basis for a claim for breach of contract or more likely a breach of a collateral contract.)

This rule is likely to present a real problem for George in seeking to cancel the maintenance contract on grounds of misrepresentation. Max may simply seek to argue that at the time of the contract he did indeed intend to purchase new cars from George but he has now changed his mind. That evidence, if credible, would be enough to sink a claim in misrepresentation at the first hurdle. George's only hope would be to satisfy a court that Max never had any intention to buy from George. His statement of intention immediately prior to contract was in truth a misrepresentation of fact.

STATEMENT OF LAW

A pure statement of abstract law cannot constitute a misrepresentation.[3] By way of example, a statement identifying the content of a particular piece of legislation, is a statement of law. However, a deliberate misstatement of law is interpreted by the courts as a statement of fact and constitutes a misrepresentation.

In practical terms, it can often be difficult to ascertain whether a statement is one of fact or law. For example, take the statement 'George is unmarried'. It may be a statement of fact and/or law depending upon the circumstances. On its own, it looks to be an assertion that George never went through a wedding ceremony. It is a statement of fact. If, however, the words follow on from an explanation as to how the ceremony in which George is known to have taken part was invalid, then it becomes a statement of law.[4]

If in doubt, the courts tend to regard statements of mixed law and fact, or statements capable of falling into either category, as statements of fact. Here are a couple more examples of occasions when 'statement of law defences' failed. Statements that:

O   planning permission existed for a particular use;

O   company X had the power to enter into a particular transaction

were both held to be statements of fact.

SALES TALK OR A 'MERE PUFF'?

For the purpose of attracting custom, salespeople do on occasions make vague and often exaggerated claims as part of a sales pitch or advertising campaign. Sales talk of this nature is of no legal consequence and cannot constitute a misrepresentation.[5]

SILENCE OR NON-DISCLOSURE

As a general rule, to remain silent does not amount to a misrepresentation.[6] For example, at an interview for a job as a travelling salesman, the applicant failed to disclose that he had serious motoring convictions. He passed the interview and was given the job. The employer sued for misrepresentation. The claim failed. There was no duty upon the applicant to disclose his convictions. The general rule is subject to a number of exceptions:

1   A half-truth can be a misrepresentation. For example, a shop assistant told a customer that a receipt for the cleaning of a dress which she was required to sign, excluded liability for damage to beads and sequins. In fact, the receipt excluded all liability. This was held to constitute a misrepresentation.

2   A statement may be made which is true at the time but which due to a change in circumstance later becomes false. For example, the seller of a medical practice truthfully stated to a prospective purchaser that the practice was worth £2000 per year. The seller then fell ill so that by the time the contract was signed four months later the value of the practice had fallen to almost nothing. It was held that the failure of the seller to disclose the state of affairs to the purchaser amounted to a misrepresentation.

3   In a contract of insurance there is a duty on the insured to disclose every circumstance which would influence the judgement of a prudent insurer in fixing the premium or deciding whether the insurer will take the risk.

4   Parties in a fiduciary relationship (for example, principal and agent, doctor and patient, solicitor and client) are under a duty to disclose such matters to each other.

CONDITIONS OF LIABILITY

Where a representation is not a contractual term, the innocent party will only have a right to a remedy if the representation is:

○   unambiguous;
○   material; and
○   the innocent party has relied upon the representation.

MATERIALITY

The requirement of materiality provides a filter to ensure that unimportant pre-contract statements which turn out to be false cannot be used as an excuse for a party to get out of a contract. A misrepresentation is material if 'the reasonable man' would have been influenced by it in deciding whether or not to enter into the contract.

For example, say Max had represented that all of the cars in his fleet were green. The cars that in fact came in for servicing were a variety of colours. Can George seek to cancel on the basis of this misinformation? Obviously not. The colour of the cars is not a material factor for the purposes of the maintenance contract in question.

RELIANCE

The innocent party will not be entitled to a remedy on the grounds of misrepresentation unless he relied upon the misrepresentation in making his decision to enter into the contract. The misrepresentation need not be the sole cause which induced the representee to enter into the contract but it must be one of the causes.

So there will be no remedy for misrepresentation if:

○   the representation did not come to his attention;
○   he knew that the representation was false;
○   he was uncertain as to whether the representation was true but decided to take a chance;
○   he would have entered into the contract even if he had known the true position;
○   he relied upon his own information rather than the representation.

Two examples will help to illustrate the point.

1   Parties were negotiating to purchase a mine. The purchasers were given exaggerated statements as to the earning capacity of the mine. However, the purchasers did not rely upon these figures. They brought in their own expert agents to check the figures. In error the experts approved the calculations. The court found that there was no actionable misrepresentation. The purchasers had relied upon the experts' report and not the sellers' representations.
2   An estate agent exaggerated the size of a garage in the written parti-

culars. Before purchase the buyer examined the property twice and saw the garage for himself. There was no actionable misrepresentation. The buyer had relied upon his own eyes and not upon the written particulars.[7]

TYPES OF MISREPRESENTATION

There are three classes of misrepresentation:

O   fraudulent;
O   negligent; and
O   innocent.

Once an actionable misrepresentation has been identified, it is important to ascertain which of the three categories it falls within. The remedy available to the innocent party will vary accordingly.

FRAUDULENT MISREPRESENTATION

Fraud is proven when it is shown that a false representation was made:

O   knowingly; or
O   without belief in its truth; or
O   reckless as to whether it is true or false.

From the definition you can see that however negligent a person may be, he can never be liable for fraud if his belief is honest.

NEGLIGENT MISREPRESENTATION

A negligent misrepresentation is one which is made carelessly or without reasonable grounds for believing it to be true.

INNOCENT MISREPRESENTATION

An innocent misrepresentation is a misrepresentation which is neither fraudulent nor negligent (for example, where the person making the representation has reasonable grounds for believing in its truth).

REMEDIES FOR MISREPRESENTATION

Assuming that an actionable misrepresentation is established, the innocent party has two possible remedies:

O   rescission (that is, setting aside the contract); or

O   damages.

RESCISSION

Rescission is possible whether the representation is fraudulent, negligent or innocent. Rescission for misrepresentation involves an allegation that there was a defect in the formation of the contract. The effect of rescission is to cancel the contract from the beginning (*ab initio*) and to avoid it retrospectively so that it is treated as never having existed.

The object of rescission is to put the parties back in the position they would have been in had the contract never been made. A party who rescinds for misrepresentation is treating the contract as if it never existed and therefore loses the right to claim damages for breach of contract.

The general rule is that misrepresentation makes the contract voidable (that is, capable of being set aside) at the option of the injured party. So the injured party can elect to rescind the contract if he wishes to do so. All he need do is notify the other party.

Termination of a contract for breach of contract is something different. This involves an allegation that there was a defect in the performance of the contract. The defect does not lead to the conclusion that the contract should be treated as if it had never existed. Termination for breach does not have retrospective effect. So a party who terminates for breach of contract can also claim damages for breach of contract.

Bars to rescission

The injured party will lose his right to rescind if:

O   with full knowledge of the misrepresentation and of his right to
         rescind, he elects to continue with (that is, affirm) the contract;

O   if the parties cannot be restored to their original position; or

O   where genuine third party rights have accrued.

Affirmation The injured party can lose his right to rescind if, with full knowledge of the misrepresentation and of his right to rescind he nevertheless states that he intends to continue with the contract or he does an act from which his intention can be implied.

This rule presents another major stumbling block for George. If the representation made by Max to buy cars from George induced George to enter into the maintenance contract, then George should have considered calling the maintenance contract to a halt just as soon as Max started buying cars from elsewhere. By continuing with the contract, George has lost his right to rescind.

Lapse of time may be evidence of affirmation. Where the misrepresentation is fraudulent, the time which is evidence of affirmation runs from the time when the fraud was, or with reasonable diligence could have been, discovered. However, although the general rule is that there can be no affirmation without knowledge that there has indeed been a misrepresentation, there is some authority that in the case of non-fraudulent misrepresentation, time runs from the date of the contract, not the date of discovery of the misrepresentation.

If restitution is impossible The purpose of rescission is to put the parties back into their original position. So rescission and restitution go hand in hand. Rescission will not be a viable option unless substantial restitution is possible. So, for example, a buyer loses his right to rescind if by the time that he wants to rescind, the goods that he bought under the contract have already been substantially altered.

With a contract for the sale of goods it should be relatively straightforward to ascertain whether substantial restitution is possible. However, can an innocent party rescind a partly performed contract for services? How is restitution possible?

This is an area that has caused the courts problems. One practical solution is to treat the contract as rescinded for the future, leaving the services already rendered unaffected. However, this is inconsistent with the concept that rescission for misrepresentation takes the parties right back to where they would have been had the contract never been made (or, to give it its lawyers' Latin tag, it is rescinded *ab initio*). It could also result in the party who has already rendered the services going without payment if the contract was entire and the payment was only due on completion and not as the contract goes along.

The better view is that the contract is rescinded *ab initio* but that expenses incurred can be recovered by the innocent party as part of his remedy.

Third party rights If, on a sale of goods, the innocent party has already sold on the goods in question then rescission is not going to be possible. For example, A buys goods from B and B then sells them on to C. B later learns that he was induced to purchase from A by misrepresentation. Can B recover the goods from C and rescind his contract with A? The law does not permit him to do so, as the rights of the innocent third party (C) need to be protected.

DAMAGES FOR MISREPRESENTATION

The right to damages upon misrepresentation varies depending upon the nature of the misrepresentation.

Damages for fraudulent misrepresentation

If an injured party can show that he suffered loss as a result of reliance upon a fraudulent misrepresentation, then he can recover damages by way of the tort of deceit for the loss. The object is to restore the claimant to the position he would have been in had the representation not been made (that is, the amount by which the claimant is out of pocket by entering the contract).

In the case of a fraudulent misrepresentation, the innocent party can both rescind the contract *and* recover damages for deceit. The right to damages arises out of tort and does not depend upon a contractual right.

Damages for negligent misrepresentation

If the misrepresentation is negligent, the innocent party has two possible routes to recover damages:

1   If the nature of the relationship between the parties is such that one party owes a duty of care to the other (for example, where the first party was in a special relationship with the other, such as bank manager and account holder) then, in the example just given, the account holder can elect to claim damages against the bank in tort.

2   Alternatively, the innocent party can claim damages for negligent misrepresentation under Section 2(1) of the Misrepresentation Act 1967.

A claim via the Act is the more usual route and has an evidential advantage. The effect of Section 2(1) of the Misrepresentation Act 1967 is to reverse the normal burden of proof. The innocent party need not prove negligence. Rather, the other party is required to disprove his negligence.

In both cases the measure of damages is tortious and not contractual. It is the sum needed to put the innocent party in the position he would have been in had he not entered into the contract.

Because the damages do not depend upon a properly formed contract being in place, an innocent party can both rescind *and* seek to recover damages for negligent misrepresentation.

However, in the case of both innocent and negligent misrepresentation, the court has a wide discretion to refuse rescission and award damages in place of rescission (Section 2(2) Misrepresentation Act 1967). In exercising its discretion, the court will need to consider:

O   can the injured party be adequately compensated in damages?
O   what loss would be caused to the party that made the misrepresentation in allowing the contract to be rescinded?

Innocent misrepresentation and damages

The starting point is that damages cannot be claimed for an innocent misrepresentation. The remedy for innocent misrepresentation is rescission.

However, under Section 2(2) of the Act referred to above, the court has a discretion, where the injured party would be entitled to rescind, to award damages in place of rescission.

Exclusion of liability for misrepresentation

Commercial contracts often contain a clause which seeks to limit or exclude liability for misrepresentation. Here are some examples:

O   the purchaser acknowledges that he does not rely on any representations other than those contained in the agreement;

O   the purchaser is not to rely upon statements made by the seller but to satisfy himself as to their truth or accuracy;

O   the final contract represents the entire agreement between the parties and supersedes any prior agreements or negotiations;

O   all representations contained in the pre-contract documentation are statements of opinion only.

None of these clauses would protect a party guilty of fraud. However, short of fraud, the extent to which these exclusion clauses will be effective depends upon the circumstances of each case. The 1967 Act provides that a contractual term which seeks to restrict liability or remedies for pre-contract misrepresentation (as these clauses do) is not effective except to the extent that the party seeking to rely on the restriction can show it to be fair and reasonable in the circumstances.

In a recent case looking at this issue, the court held that a clause which failed to distinguish between fraudulent misrepresentations and others could never be reasonable. The clause in that case was ineffective because it failed to be reasonable as a whole.[8]

Between sophisticated business parties it should be possible to agree that the final contract sets out all the terms and that the parties contract out of liability for pre-contract innocent or negligent misrepresentations. However, there can be no guarantees that the clause will work. The safest course is to assume that all that is said at the pre-contract stage may have a bearing upon the parties' subsequent rights.[9]

The second (shorter) part of this chapter deals with what is called 'waiver'.

INTRODUCTION TO WAIVER

In practice it is common for contractual obligations in a contract to be waived. For example, a contract may provide that goods are to be delivered by the seller to the purchaser on a particular date. Delivery is late but quite possibly the later date suits both parties. The contract has technically been breached but the buyer has 'waived the breach'.

Why is it a waiver and not just an agreed variation to the contract terms? Waiver and variation are similar but there are two indicators that help to establish which has occurred:

1   No consideration is required from the party that benefits from the waiver. Consideration is required for variation of a contract.
2   A waiver can be granted after a breach of contract has occurred. A variation can only be granted prior to a breach.

WAIVER OF RIGHT TO TERMINATE

One party to a contract may, by reason of the other's breach, be entitled to terminate the contract. However, the innocent party is not obliged to terminate. Notwithstanding the breach, the innocent party may wish to press ahead with the contract. If he does so, he can still claim damages for the breach at a later stage.

So the innocent party has to make an election. Is he going to continue with the contract or terminate?

If he elects to treat the contract as continuing, he is said to have 'affirmed' the contract. If he says in no uncertain terms that he intends to press ahead with the contract, the position is straightforward. However, can affirmation be implied by his conduct? The answer is that if he does some unequivocal act from which it can be inferred that he intends to go on with the contract regardless of the breach then he has affirmed the contract and has lost his right to terminate. So, for example, if the innocent party unreservedly continues to press for performance or accept performance by the other party he will be held to have affirmed the contract. Affirmation is only possible if the innocent party has knowledge of the facts giving rise to the breach and he knows that he has a legal right to terminate.

Once the innocent party has decided to press ahead with the contract and has communicated this to the other party he cannot then change his mind and decide to terminate. However, if the breach is persistent, he may find a later opportunity to terminate if he wishes to do so. If the innocent party chooses to press ahead irrespective of one particular breach, this affirmation does not preclude him from terminating by reason of a further subsequent breach.

If the innocent party elects to press ahead, as well as affirming the contract, he is said to have 'waived' his right to terminate. The party who makes this election only abandons his right to treat the contract as terminated. He does not abandon his right to claim damages for the loss suffered as a result of the breach.

Commercial contracts often contain a 'no waiver clause'. The key element of the clause is typically to provide that failure to enforce contractual rights whether deliberately or by oversight does not constitute a waiver of the right to do so. How much protection such a clause can actually provide is open to question. The effectiveness of waiver clauses has not yet been tested by the courts.

NOTES

1   *Bisset* v. *Wilkinson* [1927] AC 177.
2   *Economides* v. *Commercial Union Assurance Co. Plc* [1998] QB 587.
3   *Beattie* v. *Ebury, Lord* (1872) LR 7 Ch. App. 777.
4   Treitel, G.H., *The Law of Contract*, 10th edn, London: Sweet and Maxwell.
5   *Dimmock* v. *Hallett* (1866) LR 7 Ch. App. 21.
6   *Ward* v. *Hobbs* (1878) 4 App. Cas. 13.
7   *Hartlelid* v. *Sawyer & McClocklin Real Estate* [1977] 5 WWR 481.
8   *Thomas Witter Ltd* v. *TBP Industries Ltd* (1996); *E.A. Grimstead & Son* v. *McGarrigan* [1999] AER (D) 1163.
9   *Inntrepreneur Pub (GL)* v. *East Crown Limited* [2000] 2 Lloyd's Rep. 611.

8

REMEDIES FOR BREACH OF CONTRACT

WHAT COULD HAPPEN IF YOU WALK AWAY?

This chapter is core to any consideration a party must give to the question: can I simply walk away from this contract?

Let us turn back to the dilemma facing George and his company Rapid Repairs. As you may recall, Rapid Repairs had contracted with Rent a Car to service and valet all hire cars belonging to Rent a Car. The service was to be provided upon request with cars to be returned within one working day of delivery. The contract has run for two years with another three to go. Rapid Repairs receives an annual fee from Rent a Car of £20 000 payable quarterly.

Unfortunately, whilst negotiating the contract, George failed to consider what might happen if the Rent a Car fleet expanded rapidly. As the result of an acquisition, the fleet has doubled overnight. Because George failed to ensure that the remuneration was calculated by reference to the size of the fleet, the profitability of the contract is bound to plummet rapidly.

George has calculated that unless Max is prepared to increase the annual fee, the contract will be loss-making for Rapid Repairs. George has tried to negotiate the terms with Max but Max is standing firm. The contract has another three years to run. To continue to make a loss for that period of time is commercially unacceptable to George.

George considers a number of issues that have been addressed in previous chapters of this book (for example, is there a contract? Is Rent a Car in breach? Did Max make any misrepresentations?). However, he can find no way out. George wants his company to simply walk away from its obligations under this contract. Why should his staff continue to devote a substantial amount of their time to working on the Rent a Car fleet for only £20 000 per year when there is plenty of business available in the town for the garage at significantly more favourable rates?

But George knows that walking away from the contract could land Rapid Repairs in court. George may have good reasons for walking away, but before making his decision, he needs to consider what options are going to be available to Rent a Car. In particular, what might it cost Rapid Repairs in damages? The financial risk of potentially substantial damages needs to be weighed up against the benefit of Rapid Repairs new-found freedom.

The remedies that are described in this chapter are some of the factors that George will need to consider in making his decision.

In this chapter we will call the party walking away from the contract 'the defendant' and the other contracting party 'the claimant'.

There are three key questions that the defendant should be considering:

1   Can a claimant get a court order to force the defendant to perform a contract? This is called an order for specific performance.

2   If the defendant cannot be forced to perform, can the claimant get an injunction to prohibit the defendant's plans?

3   Can the claimant claim damages from the defendant? If so, how will those damages be calculated?

We will now consider each of these important three remedies in turn:

O   specific performance;
O   injunctions; and
O   damages.

SPECIFIC PERFORMANCE

Specific performance is an order of the court compelling the defendant to perform his or her part of the contract.

Lawyers call this type of remedy an 'equitable discretionary remedy'. This means that it is not available as of right, but only at the discretion of the court. The remedy will only be granted where the court considers it fair to do so. The conduct and motives of both parties will be relevant factors.

In practical terms, it is frequently not possible for a claimant to get a court order to force the defendant to perform a contract. There are two main reasons for this:

1   Specific performance will not be granted if the court considers that the claimant can be adequately compensated for the breach of contract in damages.[1]

2   As a matter of both practicality and public policy, the courts are reluctant to force parties to continue to work together if the relationship between the two has clearly broken down.[2]

In the Garage Scenario, if George does decide to walk away, he can at least be assured that Max will not be able to get a court order to require Rapid Repairs to service and valet the Rent a Car fleet for the next three years. Max's application would fail both of the above tests: if nothing else, Rent a Car can be given damages (money) to pay an alternative supplier.

Here are some further examples to help illustrate these principles:

1   In breach of contract, the defendant breaks his contractual promise to sell to the claimant shares in British Telecommunications Plc. Those shares are readily available in the market. The court will not order specific performance. The claimant can be adequately compensated by buying other British Telecommunications shares in the market and recovering from the defendant the difference between the contract price and the market price by way of damages.

2   What if, by contrast, the contract is for the delivery of a unique item for which there is no substitute in the market, for example, an extremely valuable painting? In such a case, damages for failure to deliver would never be an adequate remedy. Only the original will do and the defendant will be ordered to deliver up the painting.

INJUNCTIONS

INTRODUCTION

Will the claimant be able to obtain an injunction to block or limit the defendant's plans? For example, if George, in breach of contract, has walked away from his commitments to Max, can his company then enter into a new more lucrative contract with, say, one of Max's rivals, or is that a step that could be injuncted by the court on an application by Rent a Car?

PROHIBITORY OR MANDATORY?

The easiest type of injunction for a claimant to obtain is if the defendant is about to breach an express negative promise called a 'restrictive covenant'. This type of injunction is called a 'prohibitory injunction'.

Here is an example from the leading case in this area. An opera singer agreed to sing at Drury Lane for a three-month period and not to work elsewhere during that period without the claimant's consent. She received a better offer from Covent Garden and intended abandoning the Drury Lane contract.

The judge granted Drury Lane an injunction preventing her singing elsewhere. He said that no law could force her to sing at Drury Lane against her will, but the court could stop her singing at Covent Garden because of the terms of the contract.[3]

Rapid Repairs never agreed to a restriction to work solely for Rent a Car for the duration of the contract. George has the satisfaction of knowing that Max can do nothing to interfere with his future plans.

A mandatory injunction is a court order requiring the defendant to perform a particular step. It will always be easier for a claimant to get a prohibitory injunction than a mandatory injunction. Take, for example, a developer who intends to build a sewage works near a residential area in breach of a restrictive covenant. After construction, the local residents seek a mandatory injunction for the sewage works to be demolished.

In all probability, the court will refuse to order demolition. Demolition is too draconian. However, had the residents applied to court just as soon as the first bulldozer had appeared on the land, a prohibitory injunction could well have been granted, stopping the bulldozers.

As with specific performance, an injunction is an equitable discretionary remedy. The court will need to consider the conduct and motives of both parties in reaching its decision. The court may well exercise its discretion by refusing to grant an injunction if there has been an unjustifiable delay in applying for the injunction.

Most importantly, as with specific performance, the claimant will not get his injunction if damages are an adequate remedy.

CROSS-UNDERTAKING IN DAMAGES

If the claimant is looking for an urgent injunction (as is usually the case), the court will have to decide whether or not to grant it well before a full trial of the issues and without having heard all of the evidence. To protect the defendant against a possible injustice, the court will always require the claimant to give 'an undertaking as to damages'.

The undertaking is a legally binding promise by the claimant to pay damages to the defendant if, when the case gets to full trial, the court finds that the injunction was unjustified.

If he wants an injunction, the claimant may have to give a bank guarantee or pay money into court to secure the promise. Because of the need to give an undertaking, a claimant may consider that the financial risks associated with an interlocutory injunction make it an unattractive option.

DAMAGES FOR BREACH OF CONTRACT

INTRODUCTION

Most of this chapter is devoted to the question of damages and what it might cost a party to walk away from its contractual obligations. Loss resulting from the typical kinds of breach of contract experienced in the business world can be adequately compensated by damages. In these cases neither specific performance nor injunctions are available.

THE DISTINCTION BETWEEN DAMAGES AND DEBT

There is an important distinction between a claim for payment of a debt and a claim for damages for breach of contract. How do you distinguish between these two types of claim and what is the significance of the distinction?

A contract commonly provides for the payment by one party of an agreed sum in exchange for some performance by the other. For example, goods are sold for a fixed price or work is done for an agreed remuneration. A claim for the price of the goods or for remuneration for the work done is a claim for payment of a debt and not a claim for damages. The claimant is entitled to recover neither more nor less than the debt.

In contrast, damages may be claimed from a party who has broken his contractual obligations in some other way than failure to pay a debt.

It is important for the defendant to ascertain whether the claimant has a claim for damages or for a debt or for both.

Generally speaking, a claimant has to overcome less legal hurdles when he seeks to recover a debt than when he seeks to recover damages, for the following reasons:

1   The claimant need not prove any actual loss – proof of performance on his part is enough.
2   Issues of remoteness of damage and quantification are irrelevant and are dealt with later in this chapter in relation to claims for damages. The claimant can recover no more or less than the amount of the debt.
3   The claimant has no duty to mitigate his loss.
4   The law of penalties does not apply.

Quantification (that is, how much is owed) and recovery of a debt (that is, what can you actually do to get your money) are relatively straightforward matters. The remainder of this chapter addresses the more complex issues relating to the law of damages.

DAMAGES FIXED BY CONTRACT

The contract may provide that a fixed sum is to be paid by the contract-breaker to the innocent party on breach. Such a clause has obvious advantages. The parties know the financial consequences of a breach in advance and potentially problematic issues of quantification and remoteness are avoided. Damages fixed by contract will either be classified in law as 'liquidated damages' or a 'penalty'. The key features of this important area of law are summarized below.

DAMAGES GOVERNED BY COMMON LAW

Most contracts do not expressly state what damages will be payable to the innocent party in the event of breach. The well-developed rules of common law in this area have to be applied to ascertain whether damages are payable and, if so, the quantification of those damages. In particular, the law has developed a number of rules for the purpose of limiting damages for breach of contract (these include rules relating to remoteness, causation and mitigation).

NOMINAL DAMAGES

An action for damages is always available to the claimant as of right, when a contract is broken. Contrast this with the remedies of specific performance and injunctions which (as has been seen earlier in this chapter) are discretionary remedies.

An action for damages can succeed even though:

O   the claimant has not suffered any loss; or
O   the claimant, although he has suffered loss, is unable to prove the amount of his loss.

In either event, the damages awarded might typically be, say, £1. Such a small award is known as an award for 'nominal' damages.

Take a case where a consumer has ordered from a Ford dealer a new red Ford Escort that he saw on the forecourt. He has ordered it but not yet paid for it. The Ford dealer, whether deliberately or in error, sells that same Ford Escort to another customer. The Ford dealer is in breach of contract. The evidence is that the customer can easily buy another new red Ford Escort at the same price from the same dealer or more cheaply elsewhere. In such a case, the breach will have had no adverse effect on the customer and he will be entitled to only nominal damages.

Nominal damages are regularly awarded by the courts. What is the point of these awards if the claimant has suffered no loss or has insufficient evidence to prove his loss? The answer is that the award is frequently used to establish an infringement of the claimant's legal rights and is used as a peg upon which to hang an order for costs against the defendant. Although the question of how the court decides to deal with the costs of the action is always a matter of discretion for the court, a claimant as the innocent party will typically be awarded costs against the contract-breaker, even if he recovers only nominal damages. This means that the reasonable legal costs that the claimant has had to incur can be recovered form the contract-breaker.

DAMAGES ARE COMPENSATORY

Damages are normally awarded on the basis of placing the claimant in the same financial position he would have been in had the contract been performed properly. The award of damages is based on loss to the claimant.[4] The general rule is that the loss should be assessed as at the date of the breach.

The defendant may have gained a financial advantage by pulling out of one contract and entering into another. However, the financial gain to the defendant does not affect the amount of damages to which the claimant is entitled.

Take by way of example the claim for damages that Rent a Car will have against Rapid Repairs as compensation resulting from Rapid Repair's decision to walk away from its contractual obligations. The damages will be calculated only by reference to the financial loss suffered by Rent a Car. The financial consequences of the breach for Rapid Repairs (whether beneficial or detrimental) are immaterial.

The state of the market at any one time may well determine whether the claimant has or has not suffered a financial loss. Let us return to the example of a Ford dealer. Say a customer contracted to purchase a car from the dealer. In breach of contract, the customer has refused to accept delivery of the car. The dealer has managed to find another buyer at the same price. Can the dealer recover damages from the customer?

The answer depends upon whether the supply of that type of car exceeds the demand. If it does, then the dealer has lost one profit that he would otherwise have made and he can recover damages. If, however, demand exceeds supply the dealer will recover only nominal damages since he will be able to substitute one contract with another.

Contractual damages are always compensatory and never punitive.[5] The court will not be concerned with the motive of a defendant in pulling out of a contract. Whether the defendant's breach of contract was innocent or deliberate will have no effect upon the merits of the claimant's claim or upon quantification of the damages awarded.

WHAT IS THE DEFENDANT BEING COMPENSATED FOR?

Loss of bargain

The object of damages for breach of contract is to put the claimant in the same financial position (so far as this is possible) as if the contract had been performed. In other words, the claimant is entitled to be compensated for the loss of his bargain so that his expectations arising out of or created by the contract are protected.

For example, take Max and his company Rent a Car. Max struck a commercially favourable bargain when he agreed contract terms with George.

Through no fault of his own, Max will now be deprived of the commercial benefit of his bargain as a consequence of George's decision to walk away. Subject to certain limitations which are discussed below, the law of damages allows Rent a Car to recover that loss of bargain from Rapid Repairs.

Take another example. A buyer contracts to purchase raw materials for a manufacturing process. He may expect not only to receive the goods, but also to use them for manufacturing. If the seller fails to deliver, the buyer is entitled to damages based on the value of the goods that he should have received. The buyer is also entitled to damages for loss of any profits suffered as a result of not receiving those materials.

Quantification of loss of bargain

Where a claimant wants to be put in the same position as if the contract had been performed, there are two bases of assessment:

O   difference in value; and
O   cost of cure.

Where a seller delivers goods which are not of the contract quality, the damages are typically assessed on a difference in value basis. The buyer can recover the difference between the market value of the goods delivered and the market value they would have had if goods had been in accordance with the contract.[6]

An alternative basis for assessment is to value the 'cost of cure'. A defendant who is in breach of an obligation to do building work in accordance with an agreed specification is typically liable to pay damages valued on a 'cost of cure' basis. He must pay for the cost of putting the defects right or completing the work.[7]

You will recall that in the Bakery Scenario, although the ovens were functional, there were problems with automatic baking programmes and cleaning facilities. In this case, the two methods of assessment lead to the same practical result. The diminution in value caused by the breach of warranty is probably best valued by estimating the repair costs of putting the ovens into their warranted state. In other words, the defective ovens are less valuable to the extent of the cost of cure.

How is Max going to quantify his loss of bargain now that he can no longer get his fleet valeted and serviced for £20 000 per year? After he has done what he can to mitigate his loss (presumably by taking steps to find another garage to provide this service), he must make a comparison between:

O   costs as though the contract had been performed (that is, £20 000 per year); and
O   actual (or anticipated market) costs.

The difference between the two is his loss of bargain.

Reliance loss

An alternative approach to the problem of how to compensate the innocent party is to put the claimant into the position he would have been in if the contract had never been made. On this basis, the claimant is entitled to recover from the defendant expenditure incurred upon reliance on the contract.[8] As a consequence of the breach, that expenditure has now been wasted. This loss is sometimes referred to as 'reliance loss'. The reliance loss is recoverable whether the expenditure was incurred before or after performance under the contract was due to commence.

Two examples may assist to illustrate the principle:

1   A contract provides for the seller to deliver goods to the buyer's premises. If in breach of contract the buyer refuses to accept delivery, the seller can recover the cost of delivery as a reliance loss.

2   The London office of an international software company is approached by a merchant bank to provide intensive in-house training for a two-month period on a highly specialized new accounting system. Terms are agreed and a contract is signed up. Mr Chip is an employee of the software company and works from their Los Angeles office. He is identified by both parties as the man to provide the training because he helped to design the system. In reliance upon the contract, the software company make arrangements to rent a flat for Mr Chip in London for a two-month period. Rent is paid in advance and is non-refundable. Mr Chip is flown into London. A day before he is due to start work, the bank notify the software company that they have decided to ditch the system and no longer need the training. The rental and the flight tickets are now wasted costs that were incurred by the software company in reliance upon performance of the contract. If they wish to do so, the software company could elect to recover these wasted costs from the bank.

However, by seeking to recover reliance loss, the claimant cannot recover more than he would have been entitled to if the defendant had not broken the contract.[9] Had the contract been unprofitable, quite possibly the claimant would not have recouped his own costs. Why should he be entitled to do so in the event of breach?

Once a breach has been established, the onus of proof is on the defendant to show on the balance of probabilities that the claimant would have made a loss on full performance of the contract and so would not have recouped all of his own costs.

RESTITUTION

A claim for restitution is strictly speaking not a claim for damages. However, in practical terms, because it can result in a recovery for the claimant from the defendant in the event of a breach of contract, it is appropriate to understand what restitution is and how it ties in with recovery of damages. Generally speaking, a claimant can only recover in restitution from a defendant where there has been a total failure of consideration (that is, where there has been no performance of the contract at all).[10]

Its purpose is not to compensate the claimant for a loss but to deprive the defendant of a benefit. For example, a seller is paid in advance and then fails to deliver. The buyer can make a claim in restitution to get his money back so that both parties are back in the same position as if the contract had not been made. As you can see, there is considerable overlap between restitution and reliance loss.

NO DOUBLE RECOVERY

Take a situation by which a defendant is in breach of contract and a claimant has lost profits as a consequence of that breach. The claimant has a choice as to how he wishes to frame his claim in damages.

The most favourable option is likely to be a claim against the defendant for the net loss of expected profit (that is, to put him as nearly as possible in the same financial position as he would have been in had the contract been performed). Alternatively, he may seek to recover from the defendant his reliance loss/wasted costs (that is, to put him in a position as though the contract had never been performed), but he cannot recover for both costs.

Typically a claimant who has entered into a contract that he expects to be profitable will sue for loss of profits rather than recovery of wasted costs. The damages are likely to be larger.

However, if the claimant considers that the contract may have been unprofitable so that he would not be able to show any net loss of profit, or where the contract would have been profitable but proof of loss of profit is likely to be problematic, the claimant may decide that he is on safer ground to seek to recover wasted expenditure only and to abandon any claim for loss of profit.

It is possible to combine claims for restitution, loss of bargain and reliance loss but the claimant cannot recover more than once for the same loss. For example, take the ovens which were sold by Supplier to Supermarket in our Bakery Scenario. All were of poor quality and some were delivered late. Supermarket lost out financially. Can Supermarket seek to recover both the cost of the ovens and loss of profits? The answer is no. To allow Supermarket to recover both loss of profits and the cost of the ovens is compensation twice over for the same loss. Profits could only have been generated if the cost of purchase had been incurred.

METHODS OF LIMITING DAMAGES

In certain circumstances it would be inappropriate and unfair to allow a claimant to recover from a defendant all financial loss resulting from a breach of contract. The law has therefore developed a number of rules for limiting damages for breach of contract. The rules relate to:

O   remoteness;
O   causation;
O   mitigation; and
O   penalties.

REMOTENESS OF DAMAGE

The term 'remoteness of damage' refers to the legal test to decide which types of loss caused by the breach of contract may be compensated by an award of damages. In the absence of an express clause in the contract as to how damages are to be assessed, the 'remoteness of damage test' will be applied.

A claimant may not be able to recover damages for all losses suffered resulting from the breach, as some of those losses may be considered by the Court to be too remote a consequence of the breach to be compensated by the defendant.

The claimant may recover:

O   for losses arising naturally out the breach (that is, in the ordinary course of events); or
O   for unusual losses, but only where the losses were within the reasonable contemplation of both parties at the time of making the contract.

In the Bakery Scenario, Supermarket spelled out to Supplier from the outset that delivery of the ovens was required by 10 December so that the bakeries in all five stores were up and running for the holiday period. (We have considered in Chapter 6 whether or not this deadline was a condition of the contract entitling Supermarket to reject if the deadline was missed.)

Three of the ovens were delivered on time but two were only delivered on 20 December. Supermarket considered that because of the late deliveries, two stores would have to manage without bakeries over the holiday period. It was simply too late to get these two bakeries up and running during the busy holiday period. Whether or not Supermarket has the right to reject the ovens on the grounds of late delivery, Supermarket is entitled to recover profits that it may have lost as a consequence of having only three ovens (not five) over the Christmas and New Year period. Supplier knew that the bakeries had to be up and running in advance of the holiday period and it was reasonably foreseeable that delivery on 20 December was simply too late to get the benefit of the holiday business.

Here is another example from the leading case in this area of law (dating back to 1854)[11] to illustrate the importance of the state of knowledge of the supplier.

A shaft in the claimant's mill was damaged and had to be sent to the makers at Greenwich to serve as a pattern for the production of a new one. The defendants were carriers. They agreed to carry the shaft to Greenwich but as a result of their breach of contract delivery was delayed. There was no production at the mill for several days. The claimants claimed damages in respect of loss of profits against the carriers.

The Court rejected the claim. Loss of production was not the 'natural consequence' of the delay. The Court found that the only relevant facts that were communicated by the claimants to the defendants at the time of the contract were that the article to be carried was the broken shaft of a mill and that the claimants were the millers of that mill. Those circumstances alone were insufficient for the carrier to conclude that a delay would result in loss of production. For all the defendants knew, the claimants may have had another shaft in their possession or quite possibly at the time of delivery to the carrier, all of the machinery at the mill was defective and production was not possible with or without a shaft.

The 'reasonable contemplation' test is a test of remoteness and not one of quantification. It determines whether a claimant is entitled to compensation for a particular item of loss, but not how the loss is to be translated into money terms. The issue is whether the parties ought to have contemplated a particular type of loss (that is, a 'head of damage'). The parties need not have contemplated the extent of that loss.

One more example with facts taken from another leading case![12]

The case concerned a breach of contract by the defendants in failing to delivery a boiler on time to the claimants who ran a laundry. The delivery was five months late. The claimant sued the defendant for loss of profits and those profits fell into two categories:

O   £16 a week representing the loss for typical weekly profits of the laundry (the case dates back to 1949); and

O   £262 per week representing a loss of some particularly lucrative dying contracts.

The Court of Appeal held that while the defendants were liable for losses at £16 per week, they were not liable for the loss of profits on the exceptionally lucrative contracts which the claimants had lost as a result of the delay. The defendants did not know that these contracts existed. This meant that the second category of losses were not within the reasonable contemplation of both parties when the contract was made. Had the claimants told the defendants about the dying contracts before making the contract and emphasized the need for prompt delivery, then the loss would have been within the reasonable contemplation of both parties.

CAUSATION

A claimant will not be able to recover damages from a defendant for breach of contract unless he can establish that the breach of contract was a sufficiently substantial cause of the claimant's loss.[13] The breach need not be the sole cause of the loss.[14]

For example, a builder may be technically in breach of contract because he built a roof that leaks. However, if the roof is ripped off by gale force winds, the loss suffered by the roof owner is independent of the breach. There is no causal connection between the breach of contract and the loss.

Where the loss results partly from the breach and partly from the intervening act of a third party, the party in breach is nevertheless liable for the loss if the third party's act was reasonably foreseeable. For example, if a decorator, in breach of contract, leaves a client's house unlocked, he may be partially liable to the owner for the value of goods taken by thieves.[15]

MITIGATION OF DAMAGE

The term 'mitigation' is used to encompass three basic rules:

1   The claimant cannot recover damages for any part of his loss which the claimant could have avoided by taking reasonable steps.
2   If the claimant avoids or mitigates his loss, he cannot recover for that avoided loss even if the steps taken were more than reasonable.
3   Where the claimant incurs loss and expense in taking reasonable steps, the claimant can recover that loss or expense from the defendant.

The purpose of these rules is aimed at limiting the waste of resources in society. Under the rules, the innocent party is given a firm incentive to limit the damage resulting from the breach.

A claimant must take all reasonable steps to mitigate the loss resulting from the breach.[16] Another way of looking at this duty is that the claimant can recover no more than he would have suffered if he had acted reasonably because any further damages do not reasonably follow from the defendant's breach. The result is the same whichever test is applied.

The rules may give some incentive in certain circumstances to a defendant to deliberately break a contract with the claimant. If he knows that the claimant will be able to substitute the defendant's performance without suffering any substantial loss, the defendant may decide to take on a new contract at a higher profit and pay damages on the old one.

The law relating to mitigation is relatively straightforward. The disputes in this area usually turn on the facts and whether or not reasonable steps to mitigate were taken.

Let us return to the Rent a Car example. Rent a Car were in a favourable commercial position whilst Rapid Repairs were performing. They could get their cars serviced and valeted within one working day of delivery at a fixed price of £20 000 per annum. Although George knows that his company is almost bound to be liable to pay to Rent a Car substantial damages to reflect the loss of bargain suffered by Rent a Car, the common law provides him with some degree of protection. He knows that Rent a Car have a duty to take steps to mitigate that loss. In practical terms, this means that Rent a Car will have to take reasonable steps to get their fleet valeted and serviced at a competitive price. Rent a Car cannot simply take the most expensive alternative option and seek to recover the difference from Rapid Repairs.

AVOIDABLE LOSS

Mitigation is an issue where the onus of proof is upon the defendant. He must show that the claimant ought as a reasonable man to have taken steps to mitigate his loss.

For example, take the case of an employee who in breach of his employment contract is wrongfully dismissed.[17] He is under a duty to take reasonable steps to mitigate his loss. If he unreasonably fails to take an equally profitable job that is available in the market, the employer will no doubt seek to argue that the financial loss suffered by the ex-employee was avoidable and that the ex-employee should be entitled to no more than nominal damages. The burden of proof in this regard falls upon the employer.

So the ex-employee will have his damages reduced either by his actual earnings under another contract or by the hypothetical earnings which he should reasonably have earned in some similar employment.

TIME FOR MITIGATING ACTION

After he knows or ought to have known about the breach, the claimant has a reasonable time, depending upon the circumstances of the case, to decide how best to mitigate.[18] For example, in the case of defective workmanship, the claimant may want to give the defendant a reasonable time to repair or cure the defect before he decides how best to mitigate.

OFFER BY DEFENDANT

The party who committed the breach may make an offer. The claimant may be in breach of his duty to mitigate if he fails to accept. To illustrate the point, here are two examples:

1   A claimant agrees to buy a car to be delivered on an agreed date. In breach of contract, the car cannot be delivered on that date but is offered for delivery on another date. It may be unreasonable for the claimant to refuse to mitigate his loss by accepting delivery on a later date. He is of course in any event entitled to any loss suffered resulting from the delay.[19]

2   A defendant agreed to sell the claimant 200 pieces of silk. The silk was delivered but the claimant failed to pay within 30 days as per the terms of the contract. In view of this, the defendant said that she would only deliver further supplies if the claimant paid cash on delivery. The claimant would not accept this and sued for breach of contract claiming the difference between the contract price and the then current market price for the silk. The court held that the claimant should have mitigated his loss by accepting cash on delivery terms and that the claimant was only entitled to recover the amount which he would have lost had he done so.[20]

However if the offer would cause the claimant some substantial prejudice then he is not obliged to accept. For example, a buyer of goods need not mitigate by accepting the seller's offer of goods of a lower quality even with an allowance for inferiority.[21]

Similarly an employee who has been wrongfully dismissed need not accept an offer of employment involving a reduction of status.[22] What if the employer offers the dismissed employee his job back? To mitigate his loss, is the ex-employee obliged to accept? The answer is that the ex-employee need not accept a former employer's offer to take him back, even on the original terms, if the wrongful dismissal occurred in circumstances of personal humiliation (for example, on a charge of misconduct).[23]

LOSS WHICH IS AVOIDED CANNOT BE RECOVERED

What happens if the claimant takes steps which he had no obligation to take to reduce or extinguish his loss? Can he make a recovery in respect of a potential loss?

The law will only compensate for an actual loss and not a potential loss.

RELEASE OF RESOURCES FOR OTHER USES

Where the claimant terminates on the basis of the defendant's breach, the resources of the claimant are freed up. For example, take the case referred to above of an employee who is wrongfully dismissed. Once he has lost his job, he loses his income from that employer. However he now has the freedom to fill that income loss by taking another job. He will have his damages reduced:

O   by the hypothetical wages he should reasonably have been able to earn during the relevant period elsewhere; or

O   by his actual earnings elsewhere during that period.

When a claimant terminates his contract with the defendant on the grounds of the defendant's breach, the resources which the claimant would otherwise have devoted to his performance (for example, capital, labour, skill) are typically available for use elsewhere. Even where there is no substitute project to which the claimant can be expected to devote his released resources, he is expected in practice to devote them to some other use.

ONLY NEED TO MITIGATE AFTER ACTUAL BREACH

Say, for example, a buyer says before the date of delivery that he will refuse to take goods from the seller. This is an anticipated breach of contract. The seller can:

1   accept the repudiation and bring the contract to an end; or
2   refuse to accept the repudiation and the contract continues in place.

In making the choice, the seller need not act reasonably. If the seller chooses (1), then the seller has a duty to mitigate. If the seller chooses (2), there is no duty to mitigate as the contract is still up and running.

INSURANCE

What if the injured party is insured in respect of the financial consequences of the defendant's breach? Has the claimant suffered any loss beyond, say, loss of a no claims bonus?

The position is that even though an insurance policy may prevent the claimant suffering any loss from the defendant's breach, the defendant cannot rely on that insurance payment to reduce his liability to pay damages. He remains liable to the claimant (or possibly the insurer under the law of subrogation) as if there were no policy in place.

LIQUIDATED DAMAGES AND PENALTIES

We now turn to the situation where a contract expressly provides for fixed damages to be paid in the event of breach. Such a clause has obvious advantages. The parties know the financial consequences of breach in advance and potentially problematic issues of quantification and remoteness are avoided.

However, the courts are reluctant to allow a party to use such a clause if the clause entitles him to a sum which is obviously considerably greater than his loss.

Damages fixed by contract are classified as follows:

O   penalties – which are irrecoverable; or
O   liquidated damages – which are recoverable.

EFFECTS OF THE DISTINCTION

If the damages fixed by contract are liquidated damages, the claimant can recover the stipulated sum without proof of actual loss. He can recover only the stipulated damages whether these are greater or smaller than his actual loss.

If damages fixed by contract are a penalty, the claimant cannot recover the stipulated sum, but he can recover the amount to which he would have been entitled if the contract had not contained the penalty clause.

For these reasons, it is essential to construe whether the damages fixed by contract are liquidated or a penalty.

DISTINCTION BETWEEN PENALTY AND LIQUIDATED DAMAGES

The basic rules of construction can be summarized as follows:[24]

1   A clause is penal if it is in reality a threat to compel performance. If, on the other hand, the clause is a genuine attempt by the parties to estimate in advance the loss which will result from the breach, it is a liquidated damages clause.

2   Although contract wording may refer to the words 'penalty' or 'liquidated damages', the terminology used is not conclusive. The court must decide whether the payment stipulated is in truth a penalty or liquidated damages.

3   Whether the fixed sum is a penalty or liquidated damages is a question of construction to be decided upon the terms and circumstances of each particular contract, judged at the time of making the contract, not at the time of breach.

4   The clause will be held to be a penalty if the sum stipulated is extravagant and unconscionable in comparison with the greatest loss which could conceivably be proved to have followed from the breach.

5   The clause will be a penalty if the breach consists only in not paying a sum of money and the sum stipulated is a sum greater than the sum which ought to have been paid.

6   There is a presumption that the clause is a penalty when a single lump sum is made payable on the occurrence of one or more events, irrespective of the seriousness of the breach.

7   A clause can still be a genuine pre-estimate of damage even though a precise pre-estimation is almost an impossibility. In fact it is in just such circumstances that the parties may wish to avoid quantification and remoteness problems by stipulating a fixed sum.

Where possible, the courts are reluctant to interfere with the freedom of the contracting parties. The power to strike down a clause that the parties have agreed to is designed for the sole purpose of providing relief against oppression.

The pre-estimate of damage has to be 'genuine'. This means that there has to be a serious attempt to estimate loss made in good faith, however unreasonable the pre-estimate may appear to others. In construction contracts it is fairly standard practice to find a liquidated damages clause governing delays to completion of the project. Typically, a contractor will pay to an employer a fixed amount for each week of any overrun. The damages increase with the seriousness of the breach. Such clauses with their graduated damages are typically upheld by the courts as liquidated damages.

THE SCOPE OF THE LAW ON PENALTIES

There are certain sums payable under contracts to which the law of penalties does not apply. The law on penalties is not relevant where a claimant claims an agreed sum (a debt) which is due from the defendant.

A contract may provide for payment by instalments with a provision that upon default in paying one or more instalment(s) all future instalments become immediately payable as one sum (that is, an 'acceleration' clause). Although the operation of such a clause may appear to be 'penal' the clauses are typically enforced as they do not increase the contract-breakers overall obligation. Similarly, it is not a penalty for an acceleration clause in a loan contract to provide that upon failure to pay an agreed instalment, the whole capital of the loan becomes immediately due and payable.

WITHHOLDING PAYMENTS

Typically, a penalty clause requires the contract-breaker to make a payment to the innocent party. Can a provision entitling the innocent party to withhold a payment in the event of breach also be penal? In theory, such a clause can constitute a penalty. However, in practice, the contract can achieve the same result by providing that no sum falls due until performance precisely in accordance with the terms of the contract has been completed. Clauses phrased in this fashion are unlikely to be held to be a penalty, and so should prove to be enforceable.[25]

NOTES

1   *Beswick* v. *Beswick* [1968] AC 58.
2   *Chappell* v. *The Times Newspapers* [1975] 1 WLR 482.
3   *Lumley* v. *Wagner* (1852) 1 De GM & G 604.
4   *Surrey County Council* v. *Bredero Homes* [1993] 1 WLR 1361.
5   *Perera* v. Vandiyar [1953] 1 WLR 672.
6   Sale of Goods Act 1979 s53(3) as amended by the Sale and Supply of Goods Act 1994.
7   *Calabar Properties* v. *Stitcher* [1984] 1 WLR 287.
8   *Anglia Television Limited* v. *Reed* [1972] 1 QB 60.
9   *CCC Films (London)* v. *Impact Quadrant Films* [1985] QB 16.
10   *Stocznia Gdanska SA* v. Latvian Shipping Co. [1998] 1 WLR 574.
11   *Hadley* v. *Baxendale* (1854) 9 Ex 341.
12   *Victoria Laundry (Windsor)* v. *Newman Industries* [1949] 1 All ER 997.
13   *Monarch Steamship Co. Ltd* v. *A/B Karlshamns Oljefabriker* [1949] AC 196.
14   *Galoo* v. *Bright Grahame Murray* [1994] 1 WLR 1360.
15   *Stanshie* v. *Troman* 2 KB 48.
16   *British Westinghouse Electric & Manufacturing Co.* v. *Underground Electric Rlys. Co. Of London* [1912] AC 689.
17   *Shindler* v. *Northern Raincoat Co.* [1960] 1 WLR 1038.
18   *Wroth* v. *Tyler* [1974] Ch. 30.
19   *The Solholt* [1983] 1 Lloyd's Rep. 605.
20   *Payzu* v. *Saunders* [1919] 2 KB 581.
21   *Heaven & Kesterton Ltd* v. *Establissement François Albiac & Cie* [1956] 2 Lloyd's Rep. 316.
22   *Yetton* v. *Eastwoods Froy* [1967] 1 WLR 104.
23   *Payzu* v. *Saunders* (*supra*).
24   *Dunlop Pneumatic Tyre Co. Ltd* v. *New Garage and Motor Co. Ltd* [1915] AC 79.
25   *Wadham Stringer Finance* v. *Meaney* [1981] 1 WLR 39.

9

NEGOTIATING YOUR WAY OUT

So (as we have seen in Chapter 8) walking away from a contract could be expensive. At the time of making your decision to walk away, it may not be possible for you to assess exactly what the costs will ultimately be. Where possible you should look to achieve certainty by reaching an agreement (preferably in writing) with the other party setting out the terms of the divorce. The deal may involve entering into a new contract with the same party on better terms for you than the old one; it may be a 'drop hands' settlement where both parties agree to waive claims for breach of contract against the other and to walk away.

The purpose of this chapter is not to offer advice concerning the art of negotiation. There is plenty of literature available on that topic. In any event business people are frequently both more experienced and more skilled in the art of negotiation than lawyers!

What we can offer is advice upon some legal issues that you need to be aware of when you start work on trying to negotiate a settlement. We have selected those issues that in our experience most commonly present practical problems when parties are negotiating. In this chapter we will consider:

○ the terminology of negotiation – 'without prejudice', 'subject to contract', 'heads of agreement', 'letters of intent' – what do these terms mean?

○ what is the legal consequence of offering a cheque 'in full and final settlement'?

○ what are the essential requirements of a valid compromise?

○ the effect of the civil justice reforms (the Woolf reforms) on your negotiations.

TERMINOLOGY

WITHOUT PREJUDICE

Settlement meetings are frequently expressed to be 'without prejudice' and letters of offer are often marked 'without prejudice'. What does the term mean?

It means that unless both parties subsequently agree, matters discussed at the meeting or addressed in the letter, remain confidential – they cannot be repeated in court. This device provides the parties with a useful umbrella under which to explore possible settlement without damaging their case.

The underlying purpose of the rule is one of public policy. Parties should be encouraged so far as possible to settle their disputes without having to resort to litigation. They should be encouraged to put their cards on the table, but they need to know that their openness will not be held against them at trial if negotiations are unsuccessful.

It is important to be sure in your own mind whether you intend a meeting or a letter or a telephone conversation to be a without prejudice communication or an 'open' communication. If you do not want the communication referred to at trial, your letter should be marked 'without prejudice'. A telephone conversation or meeting should be prefaced with the words 'these discussions are without prejudice and so too is any offer made during these discussions'. This type of express stipulation is always advisable.

However, genuine negotiations with a view to settlement will probably be treated as being without prejudice negotiations whether or not there has been an express stipulation. If it is clear from the surrounding circumstances that the parties were seeking to compromise the dispute, evidence of the content of those negotiations will, as a general rule, not be admissible at the trial and cannot be used to establish an admission.

You need to be aware that the 'without prejudice' tag is not a magic formula that automatically keeps the communication away from the court. It is meaningless to put it on every letter. Protection will only be available when there is a genuine attempt to reach a settlement.

Here are three examples of when the court will lift the veil of protection and consider the content of without prejudice communications:

1   When the court needs to determine whether or not the without prejudice communications have resulted in an agreed settlement. The communications are relevant not because of any admissions that may have been made but because the court needs to decide whether an offer has been made that has been accepted.

2   Threats made during without prejudice communications will not be protected. For example, in one case a defendant, during 'without prejudice' negotiations, told the claimant that if the matter went to

trial he would perjure himself if necessary and bribe witnesses to perjure themselves to defeat the claim. The Court held that the 'without prejudice' rule was never intended to protect threats of this nature.[1]

3   The fact that negotiations have taken place is admissible to explain delay in commencing or prosecuting litigation. Normally in this circumstance, the content of the discussions is not disclosed. The relevance lies in the fact that the communications took place and not in the truth of their contents.

If an offer made on a without prejudice basis is accepted by the other party, the settlement constitutes a binding contract which is not protected by privilege. So if, for example, a letter containing an offer is headed 'without prejudice', a letter accepting the offer should be written without this heading. If, however, an offer is met with a counter-offer then the 'without prejudice' umbrella should remain in place until settlement.

SUBJECT TO CONTRACT

This term is typically found on documentation and correspondence when parties are trying to negotiate a new or revised contract. It provides a useful umbrella under which to negotiate and discuss a proposed form of contract. The term means what it says. The document is subject to and dependent upon a formal contract being prepared. No legally binding agreement has yet been formed and further formalities are required before any agreement can be said to be in place.

Some of this discussion has been addressed in Chapter 2 – but it is important to restate some of the issues here, as the agreement to get out of a contract can be every bit as important as the agreement to get into it.

HEADS OF AGREEMENT

Fairly frequently towards the end of negotiations the parties decide to draw up 'heads of agreement' (or a statement of agreed issues). This can be a useful means by which the parties can set up the framework of a deal in writing. However, both parties need to have a clear understanding as to the status of that document. If the heads of agreement are agreed, is the document intended to record a binding agreement?

What if the heads envisage further documentation? For example, there may be a term that provides 'documentation to be drawn up and agreed between our respective lawyers'. Is the settlement immediately binding or is it only binding once the final document has been drawn up and agreed by the lawyers and then executed?

The question is one of construction with a view to ascertaining the intentions of the parties. Each case will turn on its facts. Here are three examples:

1   If the court considers that the intention of the parties was that the execution of the further document was a term of the deal, then there is no enforceable contract unless that document is executed. The contract is unenforceable because the condition requiring execution is unfulfilled.

2   In contrast, if the court considers that execution of a further document was intended as no more than an expression of the desire of the parties as to the manner in which the transaction already agreed will go through, then there is a binding contract which is enforceable whether or not the document has been executed.[2]

3   If the parties intended to draw up a further document but never got round to doing so and in the meantime one or both parties begin performing the terms or act in reliance upon the terms, then that conduct may be persuasive evidence that there is a contract in place.[3]

LETTERS OF INTENT

You may have come across 'letters of intent'. Typically such letters might be exchanged where parties intend to proceed with a transaction but contract documentation has not yet been drawn up.

There is no clear legal authority on the legal effect of such an exchange. The use of the word 'intent' tends to suggest that the letters are no more than a statement of the parties' intention at a particular point in time. This falls well short of a commitment to undertake contractual obligations. However, unless the language of the letters suggests that there was no intention to create legal relations, there must be a risk that the parties will be bound by the terms of the letters.

Although it is dangerous to generalize, in most cases heads of agreement and the exchange of letters of intent do not amount to a binding contract. There is no intention to create legal relations. They are usually only a stepping stone on the route to a binding contract.

However, you can see the potential dangers that may arise. To avoid uncertainty, we consider that it is best practice to ensure that no binding settlement is concluded until the final settlement documentation has been signed off. This is particularly important if you want the final documentation to be drawn up by your solicitor.

A CHEQUE SENT 'IN FULL AND FINAL SETTLEMENT'

A tactic that is frequently used when negotiations are stalling is for one party to send to the other a cheque for a sum less than the full amount of the claim expressed to be 'in full and final settlement'.

If the recipient does not wish to accept the offer, can he bank the cheque and treat the money as having been banked 'on account' of his claim?

In the USA, the position is clear. If the recipient banks the cheque, the dispute is settled and the recipient cannot go back and ask for more. Lawyers have argued that a similar rule applies (or should apply) in the English law.

However, the rule has been rejected twice by the Court of Appeal.[4] The English judges consider that there are analytical and conceptual difficulties with the rule. Banking the cheque under principles of English contract law could only be in full and final settlement if there was an agreement between both payer and payee that the payee will, for valuable consideration, accept a sum less than the amount of his claim. If the payee at the very moment of paying in the cheque makes clear that he is not assenting to the condition imposed by the payer, how can it be said that, objectively, he has accepted the payer's offer?

The English approach is to look at all the circumstances and to assess whether a true agreement has been reached between the parties. Each case turns on its facts. However, the approach of the English courts can, in simple terms, be summarized as follows:

1   If the recipient having received the cheque presents it for payment without any objection or qualification, he will be taken to have intended to accept the offer and he cannot recover any more from the paying party.

2   If the receiving party presents the cheque but with a qualification (for example, 'we are accepting it on account of our claim'), then the cheque has not been accepted in full and final settlement, and the receiving party can seek to recover the balance of the claim from the paying party.

The US rule has the attraction of certainty which is particularly useful in commercial dealings. The English courts, however, have preferred to adopt a flexible approach adopting basic contract law principles of accord and satisfaction. One of the justifications for the English approach is to deter a debtor from taking unfair advantage of a creditor of modest means. The tactic of offering a cheque in full and final settlement is often used when a debtor wants to impose financial pressure upon a creditor. It can be particularly effective if the creditor is, say, a small business which is dependent on a good cash flow. The English approach provides the creditor with an option to bank the cheque on qualified terms which US law does not allow.

So while the practice may be tactically wise in the USA, there are obvious risks in England. By sending a cheque 'in full and final settlement' you may end up making a payment on account to your opposite number. You may then be tempted to cancel the cheque. But this is unlikely to provide a way out of the problem. There are only very limited defences to a claim in respect of a dishonoured cheque.

THE ESSENTIAL REQUIREMENTS OF A VALID COMPROMISE

Hopefully, your negotiations will have concluded satisfactorily and you will have negotiated a 'settlement' or a 'compromise' or an 'agreement'. In other words, you have concluded a contract. The ordinary principles of contract law apply. The settlement will not be binding upon the parties unless the four essential ingredients of a contract are present:

O   offer and acceptance;
O   consideration;
O   the parties intend to create legal relations; and
O   the terms are sufficiently complete and certain.

These are all issues that were addressed in Chapter 2. When you are negotiating and looking to tie up a deal, you need to bear in mind all of these essential requirements. In some cases certain formalities may have to be observed (for example, compromises involving the sale of land or guarantees need to be in writing).

If your negotiations have been lengthy, you may find yourself finalizing terms late at night after an exhausting day. Try to focus on the essentials:

1   Have the parties agreed on the essential terms of the deal? If not, have you at least agreed upon a reasonably certain method by which outstanding issues are to be determined? Without these minimum requirements there is no contract.
2   Are the terms sufficiently clear and unambiguous? Try to reduce the risk that the parties may fall out over interpretation of the contract at a later date. If the terms are too vague there is no contract.
3   Are the terms of the deal practical and workable?
4   Is the deal no more than an agreement to agree or to negotiate? If so, it will have no legal force. But if the essential terms have been agreed, the fact that the parties have agreed to negotiate as to the remaining terms does not preclude the establishment of a contract.

THE WOOLF REFORMS

In March 1994, Lord Woolf was appointed by the Lord Chancellor to review the current rules and procedures of the civil courts of England and Wales.

The primary aim of the review was to find ways to improve access to justice by:

O   reducing the cost of litigation;
O   reducing delays; and
O   eliminating unnecessary complexities.

After two reports and wide-ranging consultation, a new set of Civil Procedure Rules (CPR) came into force in April 1999.

CONDUCT OF THE PARTIES BOTH BEFORE AND AFTER THE ISSUE OF PROCEEDINGS

One of the key features of the new civil litigation landscape is the importance placed by the courts upon the conduct of the parties both before and after the issue of proceedings. In particular, what efforts have the parties and their advisers made to try to avoid litigation, to try to settle the dispute before or after issue of proceedings, to exchange documentation and information, and to keep the costs of resolving the dispute under control (among other things)?

For the purposes of this chapter we are focusing upon pre-action conduct only. By the time proceedings have been issued, the conduct of the dispute should be in the hands of your solicitor who should be able to give you the advice that you need in this area.

CONDUCT OF THE PARTIES BEFORE THE ISSUE OF PROCEEDINGS

Your negotiations may not be successful. The parties may end up in court. The conduct of the parties prior to the issue of proceedings will come under close scrutiny and there may be a heavy penalty to pay if your conduct falls foul of the CPR.

There are a number of ways (by use of both the 'carrot' and the 'stick') that the CPR encourage parties to settle disputes. Of particular importance are the CPR in relation to:

O   pre-action protocols;
O   Part 36 offers; and
O   alternative dispute resolution (ADR).

PRE-ACTION PROTOCOLS

In his final report, Lord Woolf concluded that there needed to be a cultural change in the conduct of disputes, particularly at the pre-litigation stage. Litigation should be an option of last resort. Parties must be encouraged to exchange information and documentation early.

Lord Woolf reported that what was needed was: 'A system which enables the parties to a dispute to embark upon meaningful negotiation as soon as the possibility of litigation is identified, and ensures that as early as possible they have the relevant information to define their claims and make realistic offers to settle'.[5] The mechanism selected for achieving this is pre-action protocols and (if the matter goes to trial) careful scrutiny by the court of pre-litigation activity.

There are currently four pre-action protocols in place – in respect of claims for clinical negligence, personal injury, construction disputes and defamation. In due course it is intended that all types of proceedings will be governed by protocols. In the meantime, the Practice Direction on Pre-action Protocols provides that where there is not an applicable protocol the parties are expected to act reasonably in exchanging information and documents relevant to the claim and generally to try to avoid the necessity for the start of proceedings.

Protocols are 'codes of best practice' to be followed wherever possible. The courts will be able to treat the standards set in the protocols as the normal and reasonable steps to take before a claim is started.

WHAT STEPS MUST A PARTY TAKE TO COMPLY WITH A PROTOCOL?

Each protocol will vary depending upon the nature of the claim. However, the requirements for early exchange of documentation and information are common to all. At the time of publication, a working party has prepared a draft pre-action protocol for debt collection. In this book we are concerned with claims in contract rather than tort. Of the three pre-action protocols that are currently in place, the draft in respect of debt collection is probably closest to the type of litigation that the contract breaker may face.

We set out below the key features of the working party recommendation to illustrate the types of pre-action steps that the parties might be required to take and the order for doing so:

1   The claimant to write to proposed defendant setting out a clear summary of the facts upon which the claim is based and the amount claimed.

2   The claimant must be allowed at least seven days to reply before proceedings are issued.

3   If the defendant disputes the claim and the claimant decides that disclosure is appropriate, both parties should disclose documents relevant to the dispute that are in their possession.

4   If the claimant decides that disclosure is not appropriate, he may be required to justify his decision to the court.

5   If the defendant disputes the claim and the claimant considers that expert evidence is appropriate, he should give the other party a list

of the names of one or more experts in the relevant specialty whom he considers are suitable to instruct.

6   If the defendant agrees to a name on the list, that expert should be instructed.

7   If the defendant objects to all of the names the parties should each instruct their own expert and the court will subsequently decide whether the defendant has acted reasonably.

8   Reports should be exchanged and either party can send to the expert(s) written questions on their report.

As you can see, the proposal is that all of the parties' cards are on the table before proceedings are issued. This recommendation falls in line with the existing pre-action protocols and both the spirit and the word of the CPR.

This new emphasis upon the importance of preparation and pre-action conduct is the reason why lawyers consider that from now on cases will by and large be won or lost before proceedings are issued.

SANCTIONS IF A PARTY FAILS TO COMPLY WITH PRE-ACTION PROTOCOLS

The protocols have teeth. Failure to comply can result in:

○   proceedings being stayed to allow the defendant to collect the information that he should have been provided with pre-action;

○   a costs penalty;

○   an order refusing to allow a party to call evidence from an expert if the protocol in respect of expert evidence has not been followed;

○   an order that the party in default pays money into court.

In a case decided shortly after the CPR came into effect,[6] Mars was severely financially penalized for having failed to exhaust pre-action dialogue with the defendant. In short, although Mars won the case, in the view of the court, Mars had behaved in a heavy-handed manner and had been too quick to issue proceedings. The penalty that Mars paid was that a large proportion of its legal costs could not be recovered from the defendant.

In order to help the courts to police compliance with the protocols, we can expect more judgements to follow along similar lines.

PRE-ACTION OFFER (CPR 36.10)

Civil Procedure Rule Part 36 replaces the old rules governing offers made 'without prejudice save as to costs' and payments into court. Part 36.10 specifically addresses offers made pre-action. In this chapter, we are assuming that by the time proceedings have been issued or are about to be issued, you will be represented by a solicitor. He or she will be able to advise as to when and if to make a Part 36 offer, and the terms of the offer. A detailed consideration of Part 36 offers is therefore outside the scope of this chapter.

However, a brief word of caution! If your negotiations are getting nowhere and there is a real concern that litigation may be imminent, you must consider whether or not to make a pre-action Part 36.10 offer. There is nothing in the CPR prohibiting a party from negotiating in whatever fashion he chooses, including by the making and acceptance of offers prior to the issue of proceedings. However, if you want to make a pre-action offer that gives you as much protection as possible on the question of costs, then make it in accordance with the provisions of CPR 36.10. The provisions are beyond the scope of this chapter.

If a party makes an offer to settle before proceedings have begun which complies with the provisions of CPR 36.10, the court 'will take the offer into account' when making an order for costs. The rule does not prescribe how the court should exercise its discretion. However, the aim of CPR 36.10 is to provide a costs incentive to the parties to make (or accept) realistic offers of settlement at the earliest possible stage of the dispute. One can expect the courts to reward and/or penalize by way of costs orders in a manner consistent with this aim.

ALTERNATIVE DISPUTE RESOLUTION

The most common form of dispute resolution is negotiation. The traditional alternative, when negotiation fails, is adjudication either by litigation in the courts or by arbitration. Alternative dispute resolution methods offer a third means of dispute resolution lying somewhere between the two.

The most common form of ADR is mediation. In order to commence ADR, all the parties need to do is to agree to the process and to appoint a mediator. The mediator's main task is to help the parties identify how best to resolve their differences. A mediator does not adjudicate between the parties in dispute or make an award or declaration.

The process is non-binding, but if a settlement is achieved the parties enter a contractual agreement which will be legally binding. The non-binding nature of the process allows parties to leave at any time. The mediator can also leave during the process if he is of the view that further efforts are not worthwhile. The freedom to withdraw, the confidential nature of the mediation and the 'without prejudice' status of offers made during the mediation are important features of mediation.

Neither the pre-action protocols nor the CPR prescribe that pre-action settlement discussions and/or mediation must take place prior to proceedings being issued. However, efforts made by the parties to resolve disputes both before and after issue of proceedings are factors to be taken into account when the court exercises its discretion in deciding the level of costs and who should pay them.

There are a variety of circumstances where ADR may be inappropriate. However, if you cannot resolve your dispute and proceedings are issued, you may have to explain to the court why ADR has not been tried.

Civil Procedure Rule 44.3 sets out the circumstances that the court must consider when exercising its discretion as to costs. Circumstances include efforts made before and during proceedings to resolve the dispute. It follows that if a party fails to offer ADR without good reason or unreasonably refuses to accept an offer of ADR, costs penalties may result.

SUMMARY

To walk away from your contractual obligations carries a financial and commercial risk. You will want to do what you can to limit and quantify that risk. One option is to try to agree terms with the other party to the contract. By all means negotiate, but take steps to protect your position during those negotiations. Consider how your 'pre-action' conduct will be viewed by the court if the negotiations break down and the matter goes to court. Finally, if you are able to agree terms, make sure that they are workable and favourable – otherwise you may need to seek advice on how to get out of a contract!

NOTES

1   *Greenwood* v. *Fitts* (1961) 29 DLR 260.

2   *Morton* v. *Morton* [1942] 1 AER 273.

3   *Smit International Singapore Pte* v. *Kurnia Dewi Shipping SA* [1997] 1 Lloyd's Rep. 552.

4   *Stour Valley Builders* v. *Stuart, The Independent,* 9 February, 1993 CA.

5   *Pereria* v. *Inspirations East Ltd* (1992) CAT 1048.

6   Lord Woolf (1996) *Access to Justice Final Report to the Lord Chancellor on the Civil Justice System in England and Wales,* London: HMSO.

7   *Mars UK Limited* v. *Teknowledge Limited (No. 2)* TLR 8 July 1999.

10
POST-TERMINATION ISSUES

Previous chapters have considered (among other things) the terms which may allow you to get out of an agreement and the possible consequences of breaking your agreement. In this, the last chapter, we will consider what happens after you have terminated your agreement.

Termination of an agreement is not necessarily the end of the story. Although the agreement may have been terminated, there may still be obligations under that agreement which will continue to exist after termination. There may also be issues arising out of ending the agreement which will need to be resolved.

The main examples of those continuing obligations are likely to include obligations of confidentiality (after all, the fact that the agreement has ended does not make that which was a secret while the contract was alive any less of a secret now it has ended); restrictive covenants (it is often the case that the ending of the contract is the very thing that triggers the start of a restriction on one or both of the parties); outstanding payments (why should the ending of the contract mean that money properly due and unpaid – indeed, perhaps even the non-payment of the money which triggered the termination – suddenly stops being payable?); indemnities; record-keeping; stock; third-party queries; and resolving disputes.

We will examine each of these examples.

CONFIDENTIALITY

EXPRESS CONTRACTUAL TERM

It is not unusual for agreements to contain express confidentiality clauses which are expressed to continue well beyond the contract period. The clause will usually specify what information is confidential; how it may be used; to whom it may be disclosed; and for how long it must be kept confidential. The basic rule in relation to confidentiality is that if something really is a secret, it can be covered by an express obligation of confidentiality.

Here is an example of such a clause, using plain English: 'The formula is confidential; you may use it only to make the product; don't disclose it to anyone; and keep it secret forever.'

IMPLIED DUTY OF CONFIDENTIALITY

Even if no express term is included, confidentiality may be implied. For example, in a contract between a solicitor and his client, the solicitor has an implied duty not to disclose any confidential information about the client's affairs, even if the client changes solicitors. An employee also owes an implied duty of confidence to his employer.

DURATION

How long the confidentiality obligation lasts will vary. This depends on the nature of the information and the nature of the relationship. For example, termination of employment ends an employee's duty of confidentiality for information which has become part of his or her general skill and knowledge. But it does not do so for information which is sufficiently confidential to amount to a trade secret. In general, though, a duty of confidentiality will not continue once the information has ceased to be confidential – in other words, once it is in the 'public domain'.

RESTRICTIVE COVENANTS

Commercial agreements frequently include restrictive covenants which are expressed to continue after termination or expiry of the agreement, perhaps for a year or two after termination. For example, an agreement between Rapid Motors Limited and Rent a Car Limited under which Rapid Motors services, valets and repairs cars for Rent a Car could include the following clause: 'Rapid Motors will not service, valet or repair cars for any other car hire company in the UK for six months after termination of this Agreement.'

In principle, and often to the surprise of business people, the starting point under English law is that restrictive covenants are unenforceable as an illegal restraint of trade. But a restrictive covenant will be upheld if three conditions are satisfied. The first condition that must be met is that the restrictive covenant is not an outright ban on competition. Second, the restriction must be necessary to protect a legitimate interest of the party benefiting from the restriction and, third, any restriction must be reasonable in the interests of both the parties and the public, considering both the geographical area covered and its duration.

It is not possible to give specific guidelines on what is reasonable – it all depends on the facts of the case. Far too often, the parties each want to carve out too extensive a space in which the other is not permitted to do business of any kind, for too long a time – the (perhaps unfortunate) truth is that a shorter, narrower restriction might actually be enforceable, and the wider, 'all-singing, all-dancing' one can fail, leaving the party free to do whatever it wants.

As a general rule, though, restrictive covenants imposed on the seller of a business are more likely to be enforceable than those imposed on employees, since a purchaser has a legitimate interest in protecting what he has paid for.

Restrictive covenants are generally construed strictly, with any ambiguities being resolved against the person trying to enforce them.

If your breach led to termination by the other party, you generally will not be able to enforce a restrictive covenant on the other party. So, an employee who has been wrongfully dismissed will be freed from restrictive covenants in his employment contract. This principle was upheld in October 1996 by the Court of Appeal.[1]

The courts will not rewrite an unenforceable covenant to make it enforceable. But they will delete (or 'strike out ') offending covenants (or bits of them) from an agreement and enforce what is left, provided they do not have to rewrite the contract to do so and it does not entirely alter the scope and intention of the agreement. So, in a contract requiring payment of commission to a self-employed sales agent after termination, a provision in the contract between them making payment conditional on the former agent not competing with the defendant for one year, was held to be unenforceable as being in restraint of trade. The rest of the contract could still be enforced, because all or most of the consideration was not the non-compete clause but the provision of the agent's services.[2]

The English courts tend to adopt a fairly paternalistic view of restrictions: people who can show that the restriction seriously adversely affects their ability to earn a living will be more likely to find that the courts relieve them of the burden of complying with a restrictive covenant.

OUTSTANDING PAYMENTS

Money may be due under the agreement in relation to the period before termination. Examples of the types of payments that might be due would include commissions, salary, royalties, fees, or reimbursement of expenses. In general, these must still be paid, even if the agreement has terminated, as long as the obligation to pay arose before termination and was not itself unlawful or unenforceable. (One type of payment that might be unenforceable would be payment for proscribed drugs, but commercial agreements would, generally, remain payable.) Many commercial agreements will include a clause to make this clear – generally by stating words along the lines that termination is 'without prejudice to' (that is, does not affect) rights arising before termination. So, if Rapid Motors terminates its agreement with Rent a Car, Rent a Car will still have to pay Rapid Motors everything which Rent a Car owed Rapid Motors immediately before termination.

INDEMNITIES

The agreement might have included indemnities against, for example, product liability claims, intellectual property infringements or tax liabilities.

These indemnities are promises to reimburse the other party in certain specified events. These could become effective after termination where they relate to matters arising before termination.

For example, if Manufacturer makes ovens and sells them to Supplier, Manufacturer may promise to repay Supplier any damages Supplier has to pay if any of the ovens injure the user – such as an employee of one of Supplier's customers. This is known as a product liability indemnity. The ovens may be in use for years to come, so defects leading to claims under the indemnity may not come to light for some time. Other types of indemnity increasingly found in commercial contracts, and particularly those involving technology of any description, are to cover the other party for losses, claims and expenses arising from claims that the thing supplied infringes in some way a third party's intellectual property rights, such as copyright, trade marks and patents.

RECORD-KEEPING

The need to make payments after termination brings us on to the next issue: record-keeping. If proper records are not made and preserved after termination, the amounts payable or paid will be open to dispute.

In any event, a claim for breach of contract or tort can be made up to six years after the relevant event. So can tax claims. If records have been lost or destroyed, then proving (or disputing) that claim will be much harder. All necessary records should therefore be kept after termination – preferably for at least six years. If the contract was executed as a deed, then claims can be made up to 12 years later. We are not addressing here in any detail what, from a legal perspective, makes a document a deed – suffice it to say that words such as 'executed as a deed' should give the parties a good indication!

STOCK

Often, when an agreement is terminated, one party will still have stocks of relevant products. A supplier may hold products, intended for the buyer, which have not yet been delivered. A distributor may hold stocks of unsold products.

The same applies to a licensee of a trade mark – when the licence ends, the licensor will want to know what is to happen to old stocks (and unfinished products) and will wish to preserve the goodwill attached to its mark.

For example, if a caterer terminates its agreement with its supplier of jam, the supplier will probably hold unsold stocks of the jam on termination. If the jars or labels have the caterer's name on, the caterer will be unlikely to want them to be sold to third parties. The supplier or licensee will, of course, wish to receive a fair price for the stock, or to retain the right to sell them on the open market – if necessary, once they have been relabelled.

If the agreement is silent on the point, the parties will need to agree how to resolve the issue. The new supplier or licensee might agree to buy the old supplier's or licensee's stock at cost price (or market value if lower) or the old supplier might be given a period during which to sell off old stocks. The key – as with all these points – is to address the issue, preferably at the time the contract is entered into, but if that opportunity has long gone, then, at least, in any negotiations surrounding the termination of the agreement.

THIRD-PARTY QUERIES

A similar issue arises in relation to third-party queries – especially new business enquiries – which arise after termination. (In other words, the fact that your agreement with your supplier has ended, does not mean that the whole world knows, and you are likely to keep receiving letters and calls asking for produce that you can no longer get.) Again, it is best if these issues are dealt with expressly in the agreement. If they are not, the parties need to agree how these will be dealt with after termination. For example, will an old distributor or licensee refer requests for new business to a new distributor or licensee? Who owns or has the right to use customer lists?

RESOLVING DISPUTES

Disputes about an agreement which arise after its termination will still have to be dealt with under the rules set out in that agreement – such as an obligation to refer all disputes to arbitration. These rules will (in a well-drafted agreement) make clear which country's law applies to that agreement and how and where disputes are to be resolved – for example, in the English courts.

CONCLUSIONS

There are, therefore, three essential points to remember when you terminate an agreement: identify the issues which will arise on, or after, termination; plan how to deal with them; and reach agreement on them where necessary.

A well-drafted agreement will identify and deal with these issues – because planning at the beginning saves a lot of aggravation later. As we have just seen, termination is not necessarily the end of the story.

NOTES

1   *Rock Refrigeration* v. *Jones* [1997] 1 All ER 1, (CA).
2   *Marshall* v. *N M Financial Management Ltd* [1997] 1 WLR 1527.

CASES IN BOOK

BIBLIOGRAPHY

COMPETITION LAW

Lindrup, G. (2000), *Competition Law Handbook*, London, Edinburgh and Dublin: Butterworths.

Freeman P. and Whish R. (eds) (2000), *Butterworths Competition Law*, 36th edn, London: Butterworths.

CONTRACT LAW

Beale, H. G. (ed.) (1999), *Chitty on Contracts*, 28th edn, London: Sweet & Maxwell.

Treitel, G. H. (1999), *The Law of Contract*, 10th edn, London: Sweet & Maxwell.

Lord Woolf (1996) *Access to Justice: Final Report to the Lord Chancellor on the Civil Justice System in England and Wales*, London: HMSO.

DAMAGES

McGregor, H. (1997), *McGregor on Damages*, 15th edn, London: Sweet & Maxwell.

INSOLVENCY

Lightman, G. and Moss, G. (1994), *The Law of Receivers of Companies*, 2nd edn, London: Sweet & Maxwell.

Lawson, S. A. (update 2000), *Individual Voluntary Arrangements*, Bristol: Jordans.

Marks, D. (ed.) (2000), *Tolley's Insolvency Law*, 10th edn, Surrey: Tolleys.

INDEX